Middle School World Geography

Focus on Economics

Curt Anderson

Bonnie T. Meszaros

Mary Lynn Reiser

NCEE

National Council on Economic Education

Acknowledgments

AUTHORS:

Curt Anderson
Director
Center for Economic Education
University of Minnesota, Duluth

Bonnie T. Meszaros
Associate Director
Center for Economic Education
and Entrepreneurship
University of Delaware

Mary Lynn Reiser
Associate Director
Center for Economic Education
University of Nebraska – Omaha

PROJECT DIRECTOR:
Mary C. Suiter
Director, Center for Entrepreneurship
and Economic Education
University of Missouri – St. Louis

PROJECT EDITOR:
Melinda Patterson Grenier

DESIGN:
Karl Hartig

ILLUSTRATION:
Roger Roth

REVIEWERS:

Patricia Moses
Golden West Middle School
Fairfield, Calif.

Rebecca Reed
Colonial School District
New Castle, Del.

Judith B. Ware
Teacher Consultant
Missouri Geographic Alliance
and Instructor
Fontbonne University, St. Louis, Mo.

Michael Watts
Director
Center for Economic Education
Purdue University, Ind.

Reva Weinberg
Ladue Middle School
Ladue, Mo.

FUNDING
The National Council on Economic Education
gratefully acknowledges the funding of this publication
by the **U. S. Department of Education,**
Office of Safe and Drug-Free Schools under PR Grant #Q304B030002.
Any opinions, findings, conclusions, or recommendations expressed in this publication
are those of the authors and do not necessarily reflect the view
of the U. S. Department of Education.

ISBN   1-56183-520-X

Contents

Foreword

Middle School World Geography: Focus on Economics blends the disciplines of geography and economics through meaningful classroom instruction at the middle school level. This publication offers students in U.S. and international classrooms the ability to develop content knowledge and to enhance their analytical skills by learning to view the world from two perspectives: geographic and economic. Both the economic and geographic perspectives are valuable to middle school students as they study regions of the world. This dual perspective helps students to understand the choices people make in different regions and to think critically about an increasingly interdependent global economy.

The National Council on Economic Education (NCEE) thanks Mary Suiter and her outstanding team of economic and geographic educators for developing and classroom-testing these lessons. They provide the students with active-learning experiences, which are a hallmark of NCEE lessons.

The development of this publication was undertaken as part of the Cooperative Civic Education and Economic Education Exchange Program funded by the U.S. Department of Education, Office of Safe and Drug-Free Schools under PR Grant Number Q304B030002 and conducted in coordination with the U.S. Department of State. NCEE extends its appreciation to program officer Rita Foy Moss for her support. We are grateful that the U.S. Congress had the foresight to realize the need for economic education in emerging market economies and the vision to see how an international education program such as this also could benefit teachers and students in the United States. This publication is an example of that vision.

Robert F. Duvall, Ph.D.
President and Chief Executive Officer
National Council on Economic Education

Introduction: **Why Teach Economics and Geography?**

Geography and economics were included as core subjects in the Goals 2000: Education America Act. In 1994, the Geography Education Standards Project prepared *Geography for Life: National Geography Standards, 1994*. In 1997, the National Council on Economic Education brought the economics standards project to fruition. The result of this project is the publication *Voluntary National Content Standards in Economics*. Both sets of standards emphasize the critical need for students to gain content literacy in order to perform as responsible citizens who are competent decision makers in their lives as consumers, producers, savers and investors and who act as effective participants in the global economy.

Economics is not a dismal collection of graphs, data and theories, and geography is "not a collection of arcane information" (*Geography for Life, 1994*). Both disciplines are social sciences that rely on critical-thinking skills to analyze human behavior. While each has its own vocabulary, tools, skills and technologies, there is considerable overlap. For example, both disciplines are concerned with resources and their use and distribution; both are concerned with economic growth – gross domestic product, standards of living and per capita gross domestic product – and both are concerned with trade, trade restrictions and interdependence. Additionally, both disciplines emphasize the use of the tools of social science: data, tables, charts, graphs, maps and documents.

Blending these two disciplines through meaningful classroom instruction offers students the ability to develop content knowledge and enhance their analytical skills by learning to view the world from two perspectives: geographic and economic.

The economic perspective is based on an understanding of scarcity and trade-offs. Economics focuses on how people use scarce resources to produce and exchange goods and services to satisfy people's wants. Because of scarcity, people must make choices about how best to utilize available resources. They must make choices about what to produce, how to produce and how to distribute what is produced. All of these choices involve opportunity costs, trade-offs and consequences. People develop economic systems. These systems develop rules and incentives that influence the choices people make.

Fundamental to geography is an understanding of spatial patterns and interactions of people with their environments. Where something exists or occurs and why are important dimensions of the physical world and the human activities that take place on its surface. Geography focuses on acquiring information about people, places and environments, and organizing and analyzing the information using maps and other geographic tools. Such information can be used to develop a spatial perspective. Recognizing that human activity affects the physical environment and that physical processes affect human activities also requires a geographic perspective.

Both the economic and geographic perspectives can inform middle school students as they study regions of the world. Through geography and economics, students can reflect on the choices people in these regions make about the use of resources and the choices they make about interaction with their physical world.

The world in which our students live is more crowded than ever before, people are more concerned about physical environments, the global economy is more competitive and people are far more interdependent. Understanding this world requires high levels of competency in economics and geography. What better way to provide this competence than by using high-quality lessons that emphasize content in economics and geography while providing an opportunity for critical thinking about real-world problems?

Classroom teachers are under pressure to teach more and more, yet the amount of classroom time devoted to content instruction has not increased. Teachers can meet the goal of teaching more in the same amount of time by using integrated lessons that emphasize content in economics and geography while providing an opportunity for critical thinking about real-world problems. Students often experience school in unrelated segments. As a result, they fail to see the applicability of what they learn in one discipline to what they learn in another discipline. Likewise, they fail to see the relevance of what they learn to the real world. By participating in well-designed activities that emphasize content in economics and geography while providing an opportunity for critical thinking about real-life problems, students are more likely to make significant contextual connections.

This publication includes nine high-quality lessons designed to integrate economics and geography in a meaningful way. The lessons offer an opportunity for students to work individually, to work in groups and to participate in simulations. The lessons employ visuals, graphic organizers, data, charts, maps and graphs. The students have the opportunity to read, write, compute, speak and reason. They learn important economic and geographic content, but they also use economics and geography to analyze problems.

Lesson 9, "The Cost of Ignoring Economics and Geography," offers an excellent example of the benefits of teaching economics and geography together. In this lesson, students reorganize their classroom using a map showing several companies located along a river. Students take roles in a simulation that shows the impact of dumping waste into a river. Through this simulation, students learn about the physical processes of dilution and decomposition that reduce the impact of waste in the environment. The students then determine the least-costly way to reduce this impact. Their task

is complicated when they learn that the costs of reducing waste are not the same for each company. Students use mathematics skills and apply a trial-and-error method to solve their problem.

This lesson affords students an opportunity to think critically about a real-world problem: pollution. As they consider this problem, they employ communication skills and mathematics skills. The lesson employs a map and tables, along with kinesthetic and spatial activities. Students solve problems in small groups and communicate results to the entire class. As a result of this lesson, students conclude that they must take into account both economic and geographic factors when they strive to achieve an environmental goal. Teachers charged with the task of helping students learn geography and economics while emphasizing mathematics and language arts will find that this lesson helps them meet multiple objectives.

Mary C. Suiter
Director, Center for Entrepreneurship and Economic Education
University of Missouri – St. Louis

Judith B. Ware
Teacher Consultant, Missouri Geographic Alliance and
Instructor, Fontbonne University, St. Louis

Content Standards: **Geography**

Essential Element 1:
The World in Spatial Terms

1. How to use maps and other geographic representations, tools, and technologies to acquire, process, and report information from a spatial perspective

3. How to analyze the spatial organization of people, places, and environments on Earth's surface

Essential Element 2:
Places and Regions

4. The physical and human characteristics of places

5. That people create regions to interpret Earth's complexity

Essential Element 3:
Physical Systems

7. The physical processes that shape the patterns of Earth's surface

8. The characteristics and spatial distribution of ecosystems on Earth's surface

Essential Element 4:
Human Systems

9. The characteristics, distribution, and migration of human populations on Earth's surface

11. The patterns and networks of economic interdependence on Earth's surface

12. The processes, patterns, and functions of human settlement

13. How forces of cooperation and conflict among people influence the division and control of Earth's surface

Essential Element 5:
Environment and Society

14. How human actions modify the physical environment

16. The changes that occur in the meaning, use, distribution, and importance of resources

Essential Element 6:
The Uses of Geography

18. How to apply geography to interpret the present and plan for the future

   MIDDLE SCHOOL WORLD GEOGRAPHY: FOCUS ON ECONOMICS, © NATIONAL COUNCIL ON ECONOMIC EDUCATION, NEW YORK, N.Y.

A Correlation of the Lessons with the
National Geography Standards: Geography for Life

Standards	Lesson 1	Lesson 2	Lesson 3	Lesson 4	Lesson 5	Lesson 6	Lesson 7	Lesson 8	Lesson 9
1. Spatial perspective		●	●						●
3. Analyzing the spatial organization of Earth's surface		●						●	
4. Physical and human characteristics of places	●						●	●	
5. People create and define regions		●							
7. Physical processes					●	●			●
8. Characteristics and spatial distribution of ecosystems							●		●
9. Characteristics, distribution, migration of human populations			●	●					
11. Patterns and networks of economic interdependence	●					●	●		
12. Processes, patterns and functions of human settlement				●					
13. Forces of cooperation and conflict among people				●					
14. Human actions modify the physical environment								●	●
16. Changes in meaning, use, distribution, importance of resources	●								
18. Applying geography to interpret present and plan for future									

Source: *Geography for Life: National Geography Standards*
Geography Education Standards Project, 1994

Content Standards: **Economics**

1. Scarcity: Productive resources are limited. Therefore, people cannot have all the goods and services they want; as a result, they must choose some things and give up others.

2. Marginal Cost/Marginal Benefit: Effective decision making requires comparing the additional costs of alternatives with the additional benefits. Most choices involve doing a little more or a little less of something; few choices are all-or-nothing decisions.

3. Allocation of Goods and Services: Different methods can be used to allocate goods and services. People, acting individually or collectively through government, must choose which methods to use to allocate different kinds of goods and services.

4. Role of Incentives: People respond predictably to positive and negative incentives.

5. Gains from Trade: Voluntary exchange occurs only when all participating parties expect to gain. This is true for trade among individuals or organizations within a nation, and among individuals or organizations in different nations.

6. Specialization and Trade: When individuals, regions, and nations specialize in what they can produce at the lowest cost and then trade with others, both production and consumption increase.

15. Growth: Investment in factories, machinery, new technology, and the health, education, and training of people can raise future standards of living.

16. Role of Government: There is an economic role for government to play in a market economy whenever the benefits of a government policy outweigh its costs.

Governments often provide for national defense, address environmental concerns, define and protect property rights, and attempt to make markets more competitive. Most government policies also redistribute income.

18. Macroeconomy – Income/Employment, Prices (Circular Flow and Interdependence): A nation's overall levels of income, employment, and prices are determined by the interaction of spending and production decisions made by all households, firms, government agencies, and others in the economy.

A Correlation of the Lessons with the Voluntary National Content Standards in Economics

Standards	Lesson 1	Lesson 2	Lesson 3	Lesson 4	Lesson 5	Lesson 6	Lesson 7	Lesson 8	Lesson 9
1. Scarcity	●	●			●	●	●	●	
2. Marginal cost/marginal benefit		●		●					
3. Allocation of goods and services		●							
4. Role of incentives				●					●
5. Gains from trade						●			
6. Specialization and trade						●			
15. Growth			●		●			●	
16. Role of government									●
18. Circular flow-interdependence			●		●				

Source: *Voluntary National Content Standards in Economics*
National Council on Economic Education, 1997

Lesson 1 - What Are Productive Resources?

OVERVIEW

In this lesson, the students become economic detectives and try to determine how economists categorize productive resources. Working in groups, the students sort cards into categories they create and then specify the characteristics of each category. Given a new set of characteristics, the students divide their cards into the three types of productive resources: natural resources, capital goods (resources) and human resources. The groups then select a product they use, list the productive resources used to make the product and identify each as a natural resource, human resource or capital good. The students brainstorm a list of goods they could produce with a given list of resources and explain why they must choose only one good for actual production. They select a product they could produce in a fictitious country and determine where to locate a company to produce it.

Geography: Geographers define a resource as an aspect of the physical environment that people value and use to meet a need for fuel, food and other products. This definition focuses on natural resources such as water, air, minerals, plants and animals Geographers divide natural resources into three categories: recyclable, renewable and nonrenewable. Because most of the Earth's resources are limited, geographers are concerned with how people use resources and misuse them by depleting, destroying or inefficiently using them.

Economics: Economists have a broader definition for resources. Economic resources, sometimes called productive resources, include natural resources, human resources and capital goods (resources). Scarcity exists because human wants for goods and services exceed the quantity of goods and services that individuals, governments and societies can produce using available resources. Therefore, resources have alternative uses. People must make choices so that they use these limited resources in the most efficient way possible to satisfy the greatest number of wants.

CONCEPTS

Geography
Resource
Natural resources
Renewable resources
Nonrenewable resources
Perpetual resources

Economics
Productive resources
Natural resources
Human resources
Capital goods (resources)
Scarcity

CONTENT STANDARDS

Geography
4. The physical and human characteristics of places

11. The patterns and networks of economic interdependence on Earth's surface

16. The changes that occur in the meaning, use, distribution and importance of resources

Economics
1. Scarcity: Productive resources are limited. Therefore, people cannot have all the goods and services they want; as a result, they must choose some things and give up others.

OBJECTIVES

The students will:
1. Define productive resources, natural resources, human resources, capital goods (resources) and scarcity.

2. Categorize productive resources as natural, human or capital goods.

3. Explain how scarcity of productive resources affects what is produced.

4. Explain how technology affects access to and use of resources.

5. Use a map to identify the landforms and resources of a region.

TIME REQUIRED

120 to 180 minutes

MATERIALS

1. Visuals 1.1, 1.2 and 1.3

2. One copy of Activity 1.1, cut apart so each group gets one set of six to eight cards. Be sure each group receives some natural resource cards, some human resource cards and some capital goods cards.

3. One copy of Activities 1.2, 1.3, 1.5 and 1.6 for each student

4. One copy of Activity 1.4 for each group

5. Tape

6. One large sheet of paper for each group

7. Markers

8. A transparency pen

PROCEDURE

1. Tell the students they are going to be economic detectives and try to determine how economists and geographers categorize different things.

2. Divide the students into small groups. Assign each group a number. Distribute a set of Mystery Cards, made from Activity 1.1, to each group.

3. Instruct the groups to sort their Mystery Cards into three categories and to name each category.

4. Create two columns on the board. Label one column "Group" and the other "Categories." Have the groups share their categories and give an example of one item they included in each category. Write the group responses on the board.

5. Ask why there are so many categories. *Different groups used different characteristics to categorize their items.*

6. Tell the students that economists have a specific way of categorizing. Create three columns on the board labeled "Category 1," "Category 2" and "Category 3."

7. Discuss the following:
   A. Which cards represent something that comes from nature? *Sand, zinc, water, plants, coal, trees, soil, copper, diamonds, animals* Have the students tape these cards under Category 1.
   B. Which of your cards represent people? *Plumber, sales clerk, engineer, assembly-line worker, waitress, teacher, medical technician, architect, mechanic, landscape designer* Have the students tape these cards under Category 2.
   C. Which of your cards represent goods that people make? *Stethoscope, scissors, factory, hammer, computer, delivery truck, oven, paper, telephone, calculator* Have the students tape these cards under Category 3.

8. Explain that **productive resources** are resources people use to produce goods and services. Write "Productive Resources" above the three columns on the board. Tell the students that economists divide these resources into three categories.

9. Display Visual 1.1. Tell the students **natural resources** are gifts of nature; they are present without human intervention. Ask

the students which column represents natural resources. *Column 1* Write "Natural Resources" above Column 1.

10. Tell the students that **human resources** are the quantity and quality of human effort directed toward producing goods and services. Ask which column represents human resources. *Column 2* Write "Human Resources" above Column 2.

11. Tell the students that **capital goods (resources)** are goods people produce and use to make other goods and services. Write "Capital Goods" above Column 3.

12. Explain that when people produce goods and services, they often use a mix of different types of productive resources. Display Visual 1.2. Ask the students for a list of resources they would use to produce a cheese pizza with onion and peppers. Record the answers on the visual. *Answers will vary and include flour, water, onions, green peppers, red peppers, chili peppers, cheese, tomato sauce, pizza pan, pizza maker, oven, pizza cutter.*

13. Now ask the students to identify each resource they would use to make the pizza as a natural resource, human resource or capital good. Label each with an N for natural, H for human or C for capital. *Natural resources: water, onions, all types of peppers. Human resources: pizza maker. Capital goods: flour, cheese, pizza pan, oven, pizza cutter, tomato sauce.* (**NOTE:** Some students may say tomato sauce, cheese and flour are natural resources because they come from tomatoes, milk and grain; but point out that someone must make the flour, cheese and tomato sauce.)

14. Distribute a large sheet of paper and marker to each group. Tell them to draw a picture of a good they use frequently and list the productive resources they would use to produce this good.

15. Ask the students to categorize the resources they list for their products by labeling each with an N, H or C.

16. Have the groups exchange papers. Tell them to evaluate the papers by circling any classification of resources with which they disagree and adding any resources the original group did not include.

17. Have the groups display the papers. Ask them to discuss their evaluations. Resolve any disagreements. Have the students come back together as a class.

18. Point out that all the groups used natural resources, human resources and capital goods to produce a good or service. Tell the students that these resources are limited and that people must make choices about how to use them.

19. Display Visual 1.3. Ask the students to categorize the resources in the Resource Box as natural resources, human resources and capital goods. Identify each with an N, H or C. Tell the students that they have purchased these resources and must decide what to produce. Ask what product they could make with these resources. List the students' suggestions on the visual. *Answers will vary and might include a house, skateboard ramp, birdhouse and furniture.*

20. Label the list "Wants."

21. Ask the students why they can't have all of these things. *They don't have enough resources.* Write "Resources" to the right of "Wants."

22. Point out that all producers face this problem: They have resources and many possible ways of using them. Tell the students this problem – when wants are greater than available resources – is called **scarcity**. Draw a greater-than sign (>) between the words "Wants" and "Resources." Draw an equal sign after

"Resources" and write "Scarcity." The result will look like this:

Wants > Resources = Scarcity

23. Ask the students for examples of scarcity in the classroom. *Answers will vary and might include time on the computer, books, space, art supplies.* Ask the students what they must do when they face a problem of scarcity. *Make choices.* Tell them that producers must also make choices because of resources.

24. Display Visual 1.3. Now ask the students what product they want to produce and why. *Answers will vary, but explain to the students that producers use their available resources to produce a product they think consumers will buy.*

25. Distribute a copy of Activities 1.2 and 1.3 to each student. Explain that geographers are interested in where resources are located and why. Geographers also try to determine how accessible resources are and how these resources can be distributed efficiently. Tell the students to refer to the map and the information on Activity 1.3. Ask them what physical features or landforms XLAND has. *Rivers, lake, forest, agricultural land*

26. Remind the students that natural resources are things found in and on the earth. They are gifts of nature. Some natural resources are water, land and minerals found under the land. Some natural resources are **renewable.** Renewable resources can be regenerated in nature. Another kind of renewable resource is a **perpetual** resource. Perpetual resources come from sources that are virtually inexhaustible, such as the sun, wind, waves, tides and geothermal energy. Some natural resources are **nonrenewable**: Humans cannot create them and therefore they cannot be replenished. Fossil fuels, nuclear fuels and minerals are nonrenewable resources.

27. Refer the students to the map and Activity 1.3 and discuss the following:

    A. What are the human adaptations to the landscape? *Factories, cities, towns, rural settlements, shopping malls, truck stops, dams, highways, railroads* Point out that the human adaptations include many capital goods.

    B. How are the different areas of XLAND connected? *By highways, rivers and railroads*

    C. Why would people travel from one area of XLAND to another? *Some people in smaller towns might travel to cities for goods and services not available in smaller towns. Some might travel to cities for jobs, higher education, medical care or entertainment such as museums and theater. People in the larger cities might travel to the rural area for recreation, sightseeing, visiting their families.*

28. Point out that economic activity also connects cities and towns in XLAND. This activity requires the use of natural, human and capital resources. Often people must move these resources from one part of a region to another:

    • Human resources move to find work.

    • People move natural resources from below the ground or on top of the ground to a production facility.

    • People must build capital goods using other resources they have transported.

29. As a class, brainstorm a list of products – goods and services – that the citizens of XLAND could produce by combining the natural resources and capital goods shown on the map with human resources. Write their suggestions on the board. *Possible answers include mining coal; cutting timber; generating electricity; farming; education; medical products or services; and recreational services such as skiing, hiking, canoeing on rivers or boating on the lake.*

30. Divide the students into small groups. Distribute a copy of Activity 1.4 to each group. Ask the groups to select one of the products they brainstormed in Procedure 29 and decide where they would locate a company to produce it, based on the map of XLAND and the description of XLAND on Activity 1.3. The groups should consider the availability of natural resources, human resources and capital goods; the accessibility of these resources and access to markets.

31. Allow time for the groups to work. Have each group present its decision and explain the reasoning behind it.

32. Ask the students to explain how location affects the way that people use resources. *Location can add to the cost of transporting resources to production sites or the finished product to market.*

CLOSURE

33. Use the following questions to review the key points of the lesson:

    A. What are productive resources? *The natural resources, human resources and capital goods available to produce a good or service*

    B. What are natural resources? Give an example of a natural resource. *Natural resources are gifts of nature that are present without human intervention. Examples will vary and include trees, water and animals.*

    C. What are human resources? Give an example of a human resource. *Human resources are the quantity and quality of human effort directed toward producing a good or service. Examples will vary and include mechanic, teacher, taxi driver and surgeon.*

    D. What are capital goods? Give an example of a capital good. *Capital goods are goods people produce and use to make other goods and services. Examples will vary and include machines, factories and tools.*

    E. What is scarcity? *Scarcity exists when consumer or producer wants are greater than the available resources to satisfy all these wants.*

    F. How does scarcity affect the amount of goods and services people can produce? Explain. *Resources are limited. There are not enough available resources to produce everything we want.*

    G. What are renewable resources? *Natural resources that can be regenerated in nature*

    H. What are nonrenewable resources? *Natural resources that humans cannot create and therefore cannot be replenished*

    I. How does location affect the way people use limited resources? *Location can add to the cost of transporting the resources to production sites or the finished product to market.*

ASSESSMENT

Distribute a copy of Activities 1.5 and 1.6 to each student. Review the instructions with the students. *Answers will vary depending on which products the students choose. For example, if they decide to make gourmet frozen fish steaks, they will need fish, water and land for a plant (natural resources); people to catch and process the fish and sales people to market the product (human resources); office furniture, processing equipment, boats, fishing poles and packaging (capital goods). Owensville might be a good place for the operation. Scarcity will affect the venture if there aren't enough fish to sustain the business or if the labor force in Owensville doesn't include the right types of workers.*

VISUAL 1.1
PRODUCTIVE RESOURCES

Natural Resources such as land are gifts of nature; they are present without human intervention.

Human Resources are the quantity and quality of human effort directed toward producing goods and services.

Capital Goods (Resources) are goods people produce and use to make other goods and services.

VISUAL 1.2
LARGE CHEESE PIZZA WITH ONIONS AND PEPPERS

What productive resources would you use to make this pizza?

VISUAL 1.3
PRODUCTIVE RESOURCES

Resource Box		
Lumber	Paint	Saw
Nails	Land	Carpenter

What products could be made with these resources?

ACTIVITY 1.1
MYSTERY CARDS

Zinc	Plumber
Copper	Engineer
Coal	Waitress
Water	Architect
Oven	Mechanic

ACTIVITY 1.1 (continued)
MYSTERY CARDS

Sales clerk	**Computer**
Factory	**Calculator**
Scissors	**Paper**
Delivery truck	**Telephone**
Stethoscope	**Assembly-line worker**

ACTIVITY 1.1 (continued)
MYSTERY CARDS

Sand	**Medical technician**
Plants	**Teacher**
Trees	**Landscape designer**
Soil	**Hammer**
Diamonds	**Animals**

ACTIVITY 1.2
MAP OF XLAND

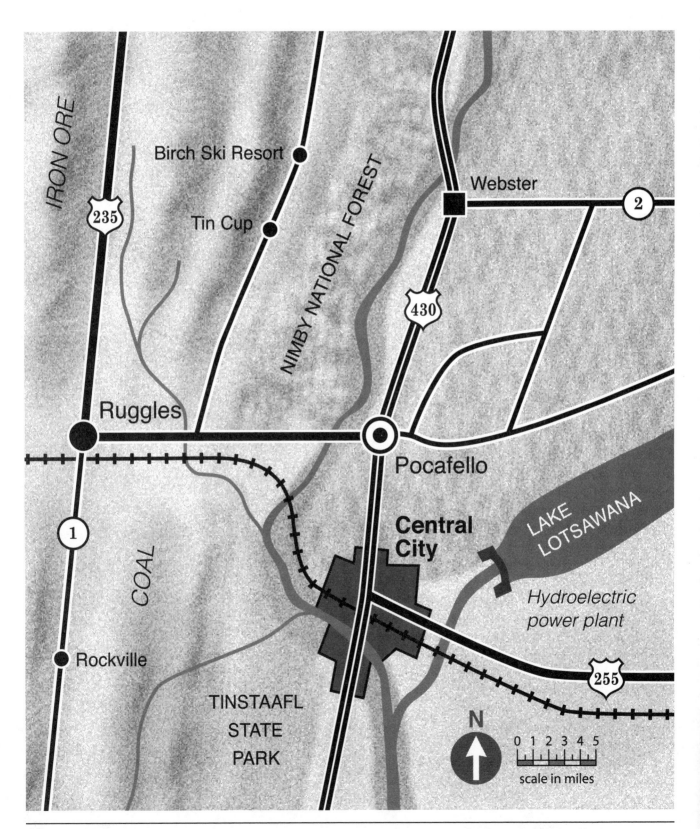

ACTIVITY 1.3
CITIES, TOWNS AND RURAL AREAS OF XLAND

Central City
- Large urban area with large industrial parks and factories
- Diverse population of 105,000
- 85% of the population has at least a high school diploma.
- Average cost of land is $60,000 per acre.
- Available transportation includes railways, highways and waterways.
- Corporation, sales and property taxes are the highest in the state.
- Offers a large public school system, private schools, art museums, theater district, science center, three universities and colleges, one community college, excellent health care with three hospitals, excellent restaurants and numerous shopping malls
- There are recreational areas nearby.

Pocafello
- Population of 26,000
- Serves as a market and transportation center for the agricultural products produced in the area
- Has a central business district with a bank, a post office, an old movie theater, a drug store, a used bookstore, a video rental store, a department store, dry cleaners, a small library, lumber and feed store, and a hardware store
- Largest employer in the town is the county courthouse.
- Wages are lower than in Central City
- Offers a medium-sized hospital, several dentists and a veterinary practice, gas stations, car dealers, self-service laundry facilities and a shopping mall
- There are no vacant buildings, and land is less expensive than in Central City.
- Sales tax, property tax and other taxes are less than in Central City.
- People have to travel to Central City to enjoy fine arts, better-quality health care and the larger shopping malls.
- The highway provides excellent connections to Central City without the pollution of the big city.
- Transportation costs to move your product will be higher here than in Central City.

ACTIVITY 1.3 (continued)
CITIES, TOWNS AND RURAL AREAS OF XLAND

Ruggles
- Located west of a river and south of two small towns: Birch Ski Resort and Tin Cup, an old mining village.
- Population is 7,000.
- Offers an educated labor force made up of people who worked at a light manufacturing plant that has closed.
- Center of town has the old train station, an old hotel used as a retirement home, a small grocery store, a tea room, a thrift shop, a convenience store and gas station, a two-person police department and a volunteer fire department
- There is only one doctor and one dentist.
- A large, new discount store is located on the edge of town across from a huge truck stop and convenience store.
- If your company locates here, the town council will provide an abandoned warehouse in exchange for the back taxes owed on the building.
- The town council will waive your property taxes for 10 years.
- Wages are lower here than in Central City or Pocafello.
- Excellent transportation options include a railroad and highways.

Webster
- Crossroads for the federal highway, State Route 2 and the river
- Farming community
- People who live on the farms go to Webster to collect mail and buy essentials from the only business, the General Store.
- Land is cheaper here than the other locations.
- Taxes and energy costs are lower here than in the other locations.

ACTIVITY 1.4
WHAT AND WHERE TO PRODUCE IN XLAND

Product _____

Use the table below to help you decide the best location to produce the product your group selected. Use the spaces to take notes and/or identify the positive and negative attributes of each location. You may add and evaluate other attributes in the spaces at the bottom. Circle the location you chose, and explain which attributes or characteristics helped you make your decision. If you need additional space, use the back of this handout.

Attribute or Characteristic	Central City	Pocafello	Ruggles	Webster
Size of location				
Available resources				
Labor force				
Capital goods				
Transportation				
Recreation/Leisure				
Access to schools				
Access to hospitals				
Access to shopping				

ACTIVITY 1.5
ASSESSMENT: Map of YLAND

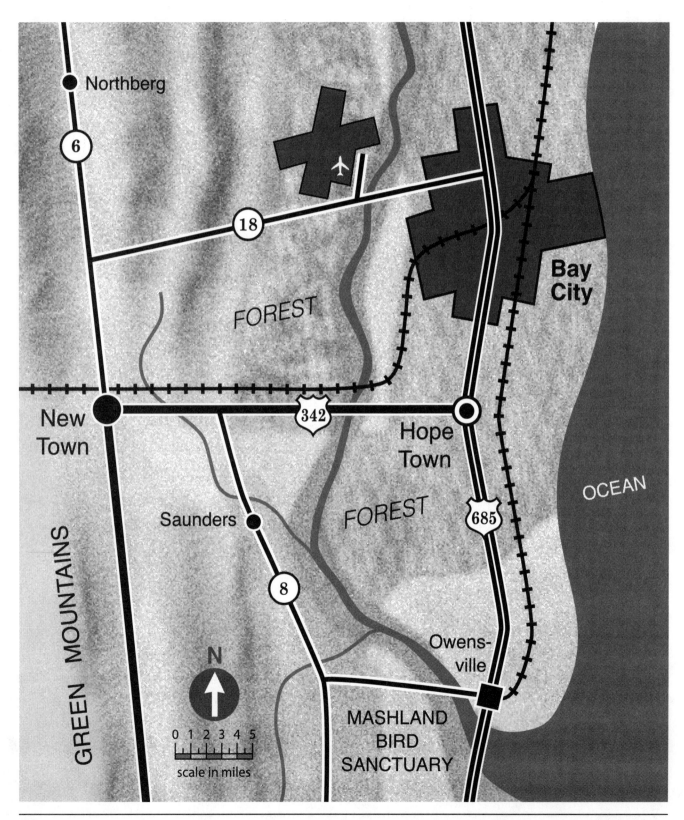

ACTIVITY 1.5 (continued)
ASSESSMENT: Cities, Towns and Rural Areas of YLAND

Bay City
- Large urban area with large industrial parks, ports and factories
- Diverse population of 650,000
- 80% of the population has at least a high school diploma.
- Average cost of land is $60,000 per acre.
- Available transportation includes one international airport with 11 airlines, five of which are commuter lines; two railroads and two bus lines.
- Sales taxes, corporation taxes and property taxes are higher than taxes in other parts of the state.
- Offers a large public school system, private schools, art museums, theater district, science center, universities, excellent health care and hospitals, excellent restaurants and many shopping malls.
- There are recreational areas nearby.

Hope Town
- Population of 50,000
- Serves as a transportation center for wood and wood products produced in the area
- Has a large central business district with several banks, a post office, a movie theater, two drug stores, a used bookstore, a video rental store, a department store, dry cleaners, a library and a lumber and hardware store
- Largest employers in the town are the lumber mills.
- Wages are lower than in Bay City.
- Has a hospital, several doctors and dentists, a veterinary practice, gas stations, car dealers, self-serve laundry facilities, a liquor store, several restaurants and cafes, and a shopping mall
- There are no vacant buildings, but land is still less expensive than land in Bay City.
- Sales tax, property tax and other taxes are less than in Bay City.
- People would have to travel to Bay City to enjoy fine arts, better-quality health care, larger shopping malls and air transportation. The highway provides excellent connections to Bay City without the daily traffic congestion.
- Transportation costs to move your product will be higher here than in Bay City.

ACTIVITY 1.5 (continued)
ASSESSMENT: Cities, Towns and Rural Areas of YLAND

New Town
- Located on the eastern slope of the mountains
- Population is 15,000.
- Offers an educated labor force made up of people who worked for a manufacturing firm
- The center of town includes the old train station, an old hotel used as a bed and breakfast, a small grocery store, a thrift shop, a convenience store and gas station, a two-person police department and a volunteer fire department.
- There is only one doctor and one dentist.
- A large discount store is located on the edge of town across from a huge truck stop and convenience store.
- If your company locates here, the town council will provide a building if you will agree to hire citizens of New Town to fill at least half the jobs.
- The town council will waive your property taxes for 10 years.
- Wages are lower here than in Bay City or Hope Town.
- Excellent transportation options include the railroad and highways.

Owensville
- Crossroads for the federal highway, a state road and the coast rail line
- This is primarily a fishing community with some businesses that supply recreational boaters with fuel and food.
- People who own the fisheries and supply shops go into town to collect mail and buy essentials from the only business: Owen's Store.
- People in Owensville must travel to New Town, Hope Town or Bay City for medical and dental care and for most amenities.
- Land is less expensive here than in the other locations.
- Taxes and energy costs are lower here than in the other locations.
- Transportation costs to move your product will be high.

ACTIVITY 1.6
ASSESSMENT: What and Where to Produce in YLAND

1. Assume you live in YLAND. Using the map and description of YLAND on Activity 1.5, list five products you could produce with the productive resources you have.

A. _____

B. _____

C. _____

D. _____

E. _____

2. Select one of the products and write it in the space below. Identify at least three natural resources, three types of human resources and five capital goods you would use to produce this product.

Product _____

Productive Resources		
Natural Resources	Human Resources	Capital Goods

ACTIVITY 1.6 (continued)
ASSESSMENT: What and Where to Produce in YLAND

3. Where in YLAND would you choose to locate a company or factory to produce this product? Use the spaces in the table below to take notes and/or identify the positive and negative attributes of each location. You may add and evaluate other attributes in the spaces at the bottom.

Attribute or Characteristic	Bay City	Hope Town	New Town	Owensville
Size of location				
Available resources				
Labor force				
Capital goods				
Transportation				
Recreation/Leisure				
Access to schools				
Access to hospitals				
Access to shopping				

4. Now, using the information in the table, determine the location for your company or factory.

5. Explain how scarcity affects what you could produce in YLAND.

Lesson 2 - How Much Depends On Where

OVERVIEW

In this lesson, the students learn how the geography of a country can influence where goods are produced. The students use a map of a fictitious country to enhance their map skills. They derive geographic information from the map, use a scale to determine distances and areas, construct isolines representing points of equal annual rainfall, identify regions and color the map to show the areas where two goods are produced. They discover how geographic characteristics can affect the production of these goods and use this knowledge to determine the opportunity cost of producing goods in various regions. The students apply this in constructing a table showing the various combinations of two goods that the people of a country can produce and where the people would need to produce these goods to obtain the greatest output.

Geography: Maps show information about the shape, size and location of places, as well as other geographic characteristics such as annual rainfall. Identifying regions is useful when people or countries make decisions (specifically, about where best to produce a good).

Economics: Because productive resources are limited, people in all nations can produce only limited amounts of goods and services. Producing more of one good or service invariably means producing less of another, and people can use the concept of opportunity cost to determine the best place to produce a good or service.

CONCEPTS

Geography
Map
Scale
Isolines
Region

Economics
Opportunity cost
Production possibilities schedules

CONTENT STANDARDS

Geography
1. How to use maps and other geographic representations, tools and technologies to acquire, process and report information from a spatial perspective

3. How to analyze the spatial organization of people, places and environments on Earth's surface

5. That people create regions to interpret Earth's complexity

Economics
1. Scarcity: Productive resources are limited. Therefore, people cannot have all the goods and services they want; as a result, they must choose some things and give up others.

2. Marginal Cost/Marginal Benefit: Effective decision-making requires comparing the additional costs of alternatives with the additional benefits.

3. Allocation of Goods and Services: Different methods can be used to allocate goods and services. People acting individually or collectively through government, must choose which methods to use to allocate different kinds of goods and services.

OBJECTIVES

The student will:

1. Derive general geographic information from a map.

2. Determine distances and areas using a given scale.

3. Define isolines and regions.

4. Define and apply the concept of opportunity cost.

5. Use a production possibilities table to determine where goods should be produced.

TIME REQUIRED

90 minutes

MATERIALS

1. Visuals 2.1, 2.2, 2.3 and 2.4 (**NOTE**: Visual 2.1 is the same as Activity 2.1, and Visual 2.2 is the same as Activity 2.2.)

2. One copy of Activities 2.1, 2.2 and 2.3 for each student

3. Enough blue, green, yellow and red pencils for each student

4. Blue, green, yellow and red transparency pens

PROCEDURE

1. Ask the students why Iowa is known for growing corn and Florida is known for growing oranges but not the other way around. *Answers will likely focus on the climate and soil differences between the two states.* Explain that these differences in the physical characteristics or the geography of the two states lead to differences in the cost of producing corn and oranges. Ask the students if it is possible to produce oranges in Iowa. *Yes, but Iowa's farmers would have to replace their cornfields with* large, heated greenhouses. *(NOTE: If the price of oranges increased enough compared with the price of corn or other crops that farmers could grow in Iowa, it might pay to grow oranges there, too.)*

2. Tell the students that the activities in this lesson will demonstrate how the geography of a country can influence where goods are produced.

3. Distribute a copy of Activity 2.1 to each student and display Visual 2.1. Explain that this is a **map** of a fictitious country called Norland. Tell them maps are diagrams that show various physical features about a country, state or region.

4. Ask the students to provide examples of information about Norland they can discover by looking at this map. For now, tell them to ignore the numbers on the map. *Answers will vary and include the general shape and size of Norland, the fact that Norland is bordered on the east by another country called Finway, that most of Norland is surrounded by an ocean and that there is a lake in Norland called Lake Omia.*

5. Explain that the map is divided into squares, or a grid, by vertical and horizontal lines that are the same distance apart. Point out the **scale** on the map. A scale is a ratio between actual measurements and the measurements on a map. On this map, the side of each square represents 10 miles. This scale shows how linear distances on the map correspond to actual distances in Norland.

6. Discuss the following:
   A. How long is Norland's border with Finway? *10 sides x 10 miles a side = 100 miles. (NOTE: Make sure the students count only the gray-shaded sides of the squares on the Finway border.)*
   B. What area does each square on the map represent? *10 miles x 10 miles =*

100 square miles

C. How large is Lake Omia? *6 1/2 squares = 650 square miles*

D. How large is Norland? *56 1/2 squares = 5,650 square miles*

E. How does this compare with the size of your state or country? *Answers will vary. Only the U.S. states of Connecticut, Delaware and Rhode Island have an area smaller than Norland. Countries smaller than Norland include Gambia, Jamaica, Lebanon, Qatar and Vanatu.*

7. Tell the students to note that there are numbers at many points on the map where two lines cross. These numbers represent the annual rainfall for that location, measured in inches per year. Give some examples to illustrate this: At the most westerly point of Lake Omia, the annual rainfall is 25 inches; while at the extreme northeastern point of Norland, the annual rainfall is only five inches.

8. Distribute blue, green, yellow and red colored pencils to each student. Tell them they will "connect the dots" by connecting all the locations (squares) using a green colored pencil where the annual rainfall is 20 inches. Tell them to follow the grid lines when locations are side-by-side. (For example, the two points just to the right of the word "Ocean" in the fourth row of the map both are labeled "20" inches. Draw a green line along the grid line that connects these two points.) Draw diagonals across squares when locations with the same rainfall are across from one another. (For example, the square above the "N" in "Norland" has two points labeled "20" inches: one in the northwest corner and one in the southeast corner. Draw a green line diagonally across the square to connect these two points.) Demonstrate by connecting the relevant points on the transparency with a green transparency pen.

9. Tell the students to repeat Procedure

8 using a yellow pencil for all locations where the annual rainfall is 10 inches and a red pencil where the annual rainfall is 30 inches.

10. Explain that the lines they drew are **isolines**. Isolines connect areas that have the same characteristic – in this case, the same amount of annual rainfall.

11. Explain that a **region** is an area with one or more characteristics in common, so the isolines divide Norland into four regions based on annual rainfall: one where the amount is greater than 30 inches, one where it is between 20 and 30 inches, one where it is between 10 and 20 inches, and one where it is less than 10 inches.

A. Have the students write an "A" in the region where the rainfall is greater than 30 inches and then lightly shade this

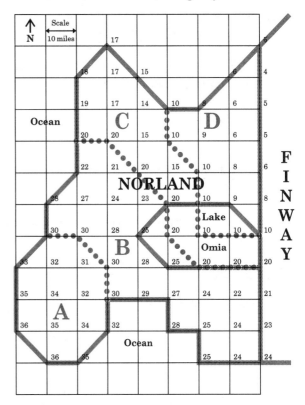

area with the red pencil.

B. Have the students write a "B" in the region where rainfall is between 20 and 30 inches and then lightly shade this area with the green pencil.

C. Have the students write a "C" in the

region where rainfall is between 10 and 20 inches and then lightly shade this area with the yellow pencil.

D. Have the students write a "D" in the region where rainfall is less than 10 inches and then lightly shade this area with the blue pencil.

E. As the students work, draw the same lines and shade in the same areas on Visual 2.1 as the students are drawing and shading in on Activity 2.1, but turn the overhead projector off first.

12. Display your completed version of Visual 2.1. Have the students check their work.

13. Tell the students that the people of Norland grow and consume two different food products: felp and bort. They would like to consume as much of both as possible but given the small size of their country, they can produce only a limited amount of each. The production of these foods requires similar kinds of equipment and human resources; but one crop requires more rainfall than the other.

14. Distribute a copy of Activity 2.2 to each student. Tell the students to use the information from Table A on the activity and the map on Activity 2.1 to answer the questions in Part 1 and complete Table B. Display Visual 2.2 and demonstrate by recording the appropriate answers in Column 1 of Table B. Tell the students to fill in Column 1 of Table B on their handouts. *Region A: 10 squares of land, Region B: 20, Region C: 10, Region D: 10* Allow time for the students to complete Table B.

15. Display Visual 2.3 with the answers to Activity 2.2. Show only Tables A and B. Allow the students to check their work. Discuss the following:

    A. Which region has the greatest amount of rainfall? *Region A*

    B. Which region has the least amount of rainfall? *Region D*

    C. Look at Table A. How does the

amount of rainfall appear to affect the production of felp? *The greater the amount of rainfall in a region, the greater the production of felp per square.*

D. What might explain why Norland isn't able to produce bort or felp in Region D? *There is not enough rainfall to support their growth.*

E. If Norland used all the land in each region to produce only felp, how much felp could it produce? *The total amount of felp that Norland can produce is 90 units or the total shown in Column 2 of Table B. The values for each region are found by multiplying the number in Column 1 of Table A by the number in Column 1 of Table B (Region A: 40 units, Region B: 40 units, Region C: 10 units and Region D: 0 units).*

F. If Norland used all the land in each region to produce only bort, how much bort could it produce? *The total amount of bort that Norland can produce is 180 units, or the total shown in Column 3 of Table B. The values for each region are found by multiplying the number in Column 2 of Table A by the number in Column 1 of Table B (Region A: 20 units, Region B: 120 units, Region C: 40 units and Region D: 0 units).*

G. If people wanted to produce 12 units of bort in Region A, how many squares of land would they need? *Six squares, because two units of bort per square x six squares = 12 units of bort*

H. If people wanted to produce 12 units of bort in Region B, how many squares of land would they need? *Two squares, because six units of bort per square x two squares = 12 units of bort*

I. How many squares of land would they need to produce 12 units of bort in Regions C and D? *Three squares in Region C. Norland cannot produce bort in Region D.*

16. Explain that the best alternative a person or country gives up to do or produce something else is called the **opportunity**

cost of the decision. For example, when a student chooses to play video games after school instead of reading a favorite book or preparing a snack, the opportunity cost of playing the games is the best alternative the student gives up – in other words, whichever activity the student would have chosen second: reading the book or preparing the snack.

17. Explain that when the people of Norland decide to use a square of land to produce bort, they lose the opportunity to produce felp. Thus, the opportunity cost of producing bort in each region is the amount of felp they must give up. Similarly, the opportunity cost of producing felp is the amount of bort they must give up.

18. Have the students refer to Table A on Activity 2.2 again. Explain that if Norland wants to produce 12 units of bort in Region A, it must use six squares of land. This means Norland cannot produce felp in these squares. For each square Norland uses to produce bort, it gives up four units of felp. To produce 12 units of bort in Region A, it gives up 24 units of felp: 6 squares x 4 units of felp per square. Discuss the following:

    A. How much felp would Norland have to give up in Region B if it produced 12 units of bort there? *4 units of felp: 2 squares x 2 units of felp per square*

    B. How much felp would Norland have to give up in Region C if it produced 12 units of bort there? *3 units of felp: 3 squares x 1 unit of felp per square*

    C. Where is the best place to produce 12 units of bort if Norland wants to give up the least amount of felp? *In Region C, because Norland gives up only three units of felp. In Region A, it gives up 24 units; and in Region B, it gives up four units.*

19. Explain that if the people of Norland use a square of land to produce felp in Region A, they can produce four units of felp, but they give up producing two units of bort.

This means they give up one-half unit of bort for every unit of felp they produce. (**NOTE:** Four units of felp equal two units of bort. To determine what one unit of felp equals, divide both sides of this equation by four to yield the following answer: One unit of felp equals one-half unit of bort.)

20. Display Visual 2.4 and discuss the following questions:

    A. What is the opportunity cost of producing one unit of felp in Region B; in other words, how much bort does Region B give up to produce one unit of felp? *It gives up three units.*

    B. What is the opportunity cost of producing one unit of felp in Region C – how much bort does Region C give up to produce one unit of felp? *Four units*

    C. Which region has the lowest opportunity cost in producing felp – in which region does it cost the least to produce felp? *Region A, because Norland gives up the smallest amount of bort for each unit of felp it produces*

    D. Which region is the second least-expensive in which to produce felp? *Region B, where Norland gives up only three units of bort, while in Region C, it would have to give up four units*

21. Tell the students to use the information from Visual 2.4 and from Tables A and B on Activity 2.2 to complete Part 2 on Activity 2.2. Explain that Column 1 of Table C shows the amount of bort Norland could produce – 180 units – if it didn't produce any felp. Ask the students how they would compute this total. *By adding the amounts in Column 3 of Table B*

22. Ask the students to imagine that Norland wants to produce 10 units of felp.

    A. In what region should Norland produce these units? Why? *The region with the lowest opportunity cost, because Norland doesn't have to give up as much bort to get some more felp*

    B. Which region has the lowest opportunity cost for producing felp? *Region A*

C. How many squares of land must Norland use in Region A to produce 10 units of felp? *Two and one-half squares, because it can produce four units of felp per square*

D. How much bort will Norland give up? *Five units: It could produce two units of bort in each square, and 2 x 2 1/2 = 5*

23. Explain that if Norland produces 10 units of felp, it gives up five units of bort. Bort production is reduced from 180 to 175. Tell the students to write 175 in Column 2 of Table C.

24. Explain that if Norland wants to produce 10 more units of felp, it should produce this additional felp in Region A. This means Norland will give up another five units of bort. Felp production now totals 20 units, but bort production has dropped again, this time to 170 units (175 − 5 = 170). Tell the students to record 170 in Column 3. Have them repeat this process for Columns 4 and 5.

25. Explain that Norland is now using all the land in Region A to produce felp. If it wants to produce more felp, it must move to another region. Discuss the following:

    A. Which region has the second-lowest opportunity cost for producing felp? *Region B*

    B. If Norland produces one unit of felp in Region B, how much bort does it give up? *Three units*

    C. How much felp can Norland produce per square of land in Region B, and how much bort does it give up? *It can produce two units of felp and will give up six units of bort per square of land.*

    D. If Norland produces 10 more units of felp, how many squares of land must it use in Region B? *Five squares: 5 x 2 units of felp per square = 10 units of felp*

    E. If Norland gives up six units of bort per square of land in Region B, how much bort will it give up in five squares of land? *30 units of bort: 6 units x 5 squares of land = 30*

26. Explain that this means felp production will increase to 50 units, but bort production will decrease to 130 units. Have the students record 130 units of bort in Column 6 of Table C. Continue working with the students using land in Region B to complete Columns 7, 8 and 9. *Column 7 is 60 felp and 100 bort. Column 8 is 70 felp and 70 bort. Column 9 is 80 felp and 40 bort.*

27. Explain that Norland is now using all of Regions A and B to produce felp. If it wants to produce 10 more units of felp, it will have to produce felp in Region C. Discuss the following:

    A. How many squares of land will Norland need in Region C to produce 10 units of felp? *Ten squares; it can produce one units of felp per square*

    B. How much bort will Norland give up? *Four units per square x 10 squares = 40 units*

    C. What amount of bort should be recorded in Column 10? *Zero units*

28. Display Table C of Visual 2.3, and have the students check to be certain that they recorded the correct information.

29. Tell the students that Table C shows the various combinations of bort and felp that Norland is able to produce with the resources it has. This is called Norland's **production possibilities**. Write "Production Possibilities for Norland" on the Title line above Table C, and have the students write the title on their handout. Note that these amounts depend on Norland producing felp and bort in the region with the lowest opportunity cost.

30. Discuss the following:

    A. As the people of Norland produce more felp, what happens to the maximum amount of bort they can produce? *It decreases.*

    B. As they produce more bort, what happens to the maximum amount of felp they can produce? *It decreases.*

31. Display the map of Norland on Visual 2.1 and note the following:
    - Region A (red): When Norland produces 40 units of felp, it uses all of Region A for felp production.
    - Region B (green): When it produces 80 units of felp, it uses all of Regions A and B.
    - Region C: When it produces 90 units of felp, it uses all of Regions A, B and C and does not produce any bort.

32. Point out that if Norland produces 40 units of felp, it can still produce 160 units of bort. But suppose that instead of producing the 40 units of felp in Region A, Norland produced the 40 units of felp in Region B. What is the greatest amount of bort that Norland could produce? *Producing 40 units of felp in Region B would require all of Region B, leaving Regions A and C for bort production. Norland could produce 20 units of bort in Region A, while it could produce 40 units in Region C. This yields a total of 60 units of bort.*

33. Ask the students how this amount compares with the amount shown in Table C of Activity 2.2. *Much less: 60 units instead of 160 units*

34. Note that *where* Norland grows felp and bort has a big impact on the amounts of felp and bort Norland can produce. By choosing regions where the opportunity cost of producing a good is the lowest, a country can produce more of all goods. Florida produces oranges because the opportunity cost of growing them there is lower than in Iowa, so the country as a whole is able to produce more oranges and more corn.

CLOSURE

35. Use the following questions to review the key points of the lesson:
    A. What kind of geographic information can we gather from a map? *Shape, location, size, directions, other physical features such as annual rainfall*
    B. What does the scale on a map show? *How distances on the map correspond to actual distances*
    C. What do isolines on a map show? *Locations that have the same amount or level of some characteristic*
    D. What is a region? *An area in which all locations share one or more common characteristics*
    E. What is the opportunity cost of doing something? *The best alternative a person or country gives up to do or produce something else*
    F. To achieve the greatest amount of production, in what type of region should a country produce a good? *Where the opportunity cost is the lowest*
    G. What does a production possibilities table show? *The various combinations of two goods that a country is able to produce with the resources it has*
    H. As the production of one good increases in a country, what must happen to the production of other goods? *Production must decrease.*
    I. Why should people consider opportunity cost when they make a production decision? *By considering opportunity cost, people choose the production of goods for which they give up the least — lowest opportunity cost — or they select the production location with the lowest opportunity cost. As a result, people in a country can get more production of all goods.*

ASSESSMENT

Distribute one copy of Activity 2.3 to each student. Tell them to use their copies of Activity 2.1 to help them complete the assessment.

PART 1

Determine the opportunity cost of producing one unit of felp in each region.

> Region A: *1/2* unit(s) of bort
> Region B: *3* unit(s) of bort
> Region C: *4* unit(s) of bort
> Region D: *1* unit(s) of bort

PART 2

Given your answers in Part 1, determine the order in which these regions should be used for felp production in order to have the smallest reduction in the amount of bort produced.

> First region: *A*
> Second region: *D*
> Third region: *B*
> Last region: *C*

PART 3

Given your answers in Parts 1 and 2, complete Table B to show the maximum amount of bort Norland could produce given the amounts of felp shown.

PART 4

For the combination in Column 7, identify the regions in which Norland must produce felp and bort to achieve 60 units of felp and 160 units of bort. *Norland would use all of Regions A and D to produce felp and all of Regions B and C to produce bort.*

PART 5

Why should people consider opportunity cost when making production decisions? *By considering opportunity cost, we choose the production of goods for which we give up the least – lowest opportunity cost – or we select the production location with the lowest opportunity cost. As a result, a country can get more production of all goods.*

Table B. New Production Possibilities for Norland

	1.	2.	3.	4.	5.	6.	7.	8.	9.	10.	11.	12.
Units of felp	0	10	20	30	40	50	60	70	80	90	100	110
Units of bort	*200*	*195*	*190*	*185*	*180*	*170*	*160*	*130*	*100*	*70*	*40*	*0*

VISUAL 2.1
MAP OF NORLAND

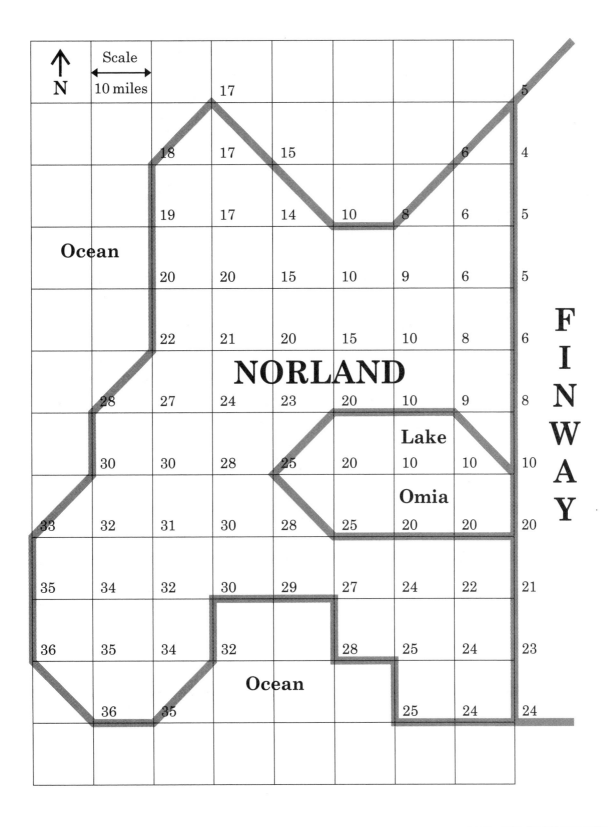

VISUAL 2.2
HOW MUCH BORT AND FELP?

Table A. Production of Felp and Bort in Norland per Square of Land

	1. Amount of Felp Per Square of Land	2. Amount of Bort Per Square of Land
Region A	4	2
Region B	2	6
Region C	1	4
Region D	0	0

PART 1
Use the information in Table A to answer the questions and complete Table B.

A. How many squares of land are available in each region of Norland? (Do not count the squares in Lake Omia; bort and felp can't be grown there!) Record your answers in Column 1 of Table B.

B. If Norland used all the land in each region to produce only felp, how much felp could it produce? To answer this question, consider the information you have in Tables A and B. Record your answer in Column 2 of Table B.

C. If Norland used all the land in each region to produce only bort, how much bort could it produce? To answer this question, consider the information you have in Tables A and B. Record your answer in Column 3 of Table B.

Table B. Total Production of Felp and Bort in Norland

	1. Total Number of Squares of Land	2. Possible Felp Production	3. Possible Bort Production
Region A			
Region B			
Region C			
Region D			
Total			

VISUAL 2.2 (continued)
HOW MUCH BORT AND FELP?

PART 2
Fill in Table C below. This table shows the greatest amount of bort that Norland could produce, assuming it is already producing the amount of felp shown. For example, if Norland produces zero units of felp, the maximum amount of bort it could produce is 180 units in all the regions. (Did you get this number in Column 3 of Table B? If not, check your work!)

To complete the rest of the table, imagine Norland wants to increase felp production 10 units at a time. Decide where Norland should produce these 10 units to have the smallest drop in bort production (Use the opportunity cost of producing felp in each region to guide you). Once you have chosen where to produce the 10 units, determine how much bort production will decrease and subtract this from the previous amount of bort. Then write your answer in the appropriate column.

Table C. _____

	1.	2.	3.	4.	5.	6.	7.	8.	9.	10.
Units of felp	0	10	20	30	40	50	60	70	80	90
Units of bort	180									

VISUAL 2.3
ANSWERS TO ACTIVITY 2.2

Table A. Production of Felp and Bort in Norland per Square of Land

	1. Amount of Felp Per Square of Land	2. Amount of Bort Per Square of Land
Region A	4	2
Region B	2	6
Region C	1	4
Region D	0	0

PART 1

Use the information in Table A to answer the questions and complete Table B.

   A. How many squares of land are available in each region of Norland? (Do not count the squares in Lake Omia; bort and felp can't be grown there!) Record your answers in Column 1 of Table B.

   B. If Norland used all the land in each region to produce only felp, how much felp could it produce? To answer this question, consider the information you have in Tables A and B. Record your answer in Column 2 of Table B.

   C. If Norland used all the land in each region to produce only bort, how much bort could it produce? To answer this question, consider the information you have in Tables A and B. Record your answer in Column 3 of Table B.

Table B. Total Production of Felp and Bort in Norland

	1. Total Number of Squares of Land	2. Possible Felp Production	3. Possible Bort Production
Region A	10	40	20
Region B	20	40	120
Region C	10	10	40
Region D	10	0	0
Total	50	90	180

VISUAL 2.3 (continued)
ANSWERS TO ACTIVITY 2.2

PART 2

Fill in Table C below. This table shows the greatest amount of bort that Norland could produce, assuming it is already producing the amount of felp shown. For example, if Norland produces zero units of felp, the maximum amount of bort it could produce is 180 units in all the regions. (Did you get this number in Column 3 of Table B? If not, check your work!)

To complete the rest of the table, imagine Norland wants to increase felp production 10 units at a time. Decide where Norland should produce these 10 units to have the smallest drop in bort production (Use the opportunity cost of producing felp in each region to guide you). Once you have chosen where to produce the 10 units, determine how much bort production will go down and subtract this from the previous amount of bort. Then write your answer in the appropriate column.

Table C. _____

	1.	2.	3.	4.	5.	6.	7.	8.	9.	10.
Units of felp	0	10	20	30	40	50	60	70	80	90
Units of bort	180	*175*	*170*	*165*	*160*	*130*	*100*	*70*	*40*	*0*

VISUAL 2.4
OPPORTUNITY COST

The Opportunity Cost of One Unit of Felp

In Region A: 1/2 unit of Bort

In Region B: 3 units of Bort

In Region C: 4 units of Bort

ACTIVITY 2.1
MAP OF NORLAND

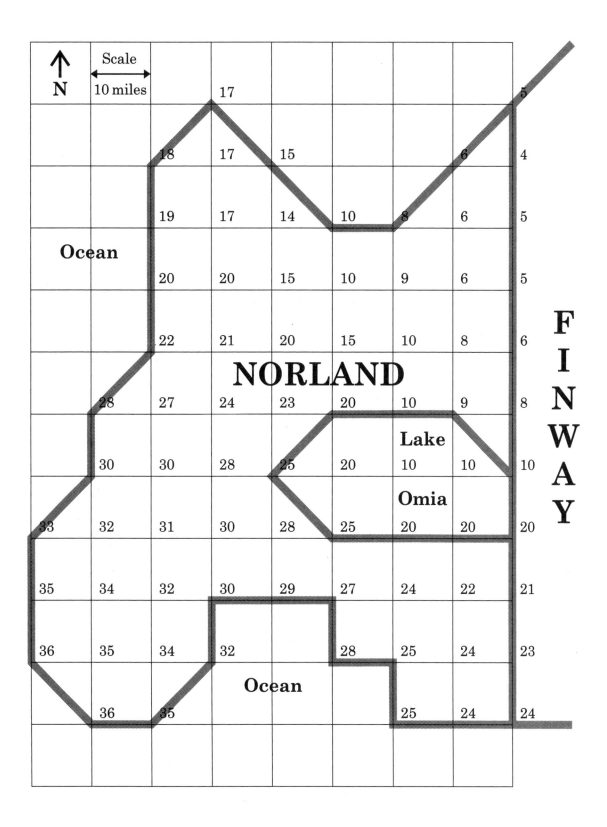

ACTIVITY 2.2
HOW MUCH BORT AND FELP?

Table A. Production of Felp and Bort in Norland per Square of Land

	1. Amount of Felp Per Square of Land	2. Amount of Bort Per Square of Land
Region A	4	2
Region B	2	6
Region C	1	4
Region D	0	0

PART 1

Use the information in Table A to answer the questions and complete Table B.

A. How many squares of land are available in each region of Norland? (Do not count the squares in Lake Omia; bort and felp can't be grown there!) Record your answers in Column 1 of Table B.

B. If Norland used all the land in each region to produce only felp, how much felp could it produce? To answer this question, consider the information you have in Tables A and B. Record your answer in Column 2 of Table B.

C. If Norland used all the land in each region to produce only bort, how much bort could it produce? To answer this question, consider the information you have in Tables A and B. Record your answer in Column 3 of Table B.

Table B. Total Production of Felp and Bort in Norland

	1. Total Number of Squares of Land	2. Possible Felp Production	3. Possible Bort Production
Region A			
Region B			
Region C			
Region D			
Total			

ACTIVITY 2.2 (continued)
HOW MUCH BORT AND FELP?

PART 2

Fill in Table C below. This table shows the greatest amount of bort that Norland could produce, assuming it is already producing the amount of felp shown. For example, if Norland produces zero units of felp, the maximum amount of bort it could produce is 180 units in all the regions. (Did you get this number in Column 3 of Table B? If not, check your work!)

To complete the rest of the table, imagine Norland wants to increase felp production 10 units at a time. Decide where Norland should produce these 10 units to have the smallest drop in bort production (Use the opportunity cost of producing felp in each region to guide you). Once you have chosen where to produce the 10 units, determine how much bort production will decrease and subtract this from the previous amount of bort. Then write your answer in the appropriate column.

Table C. _____

	1.	2.	3.	4.	5.	6.	7.	8.	9.	10.
Units of felp	0	10	20	30	40	50	60	70	80	90
Units of bort	180									

ACTIVITY 2.3
ASSESSMENT

The people of Norland recently constructed a canal system that uses excess water from Lake Omia to irrigate the land in Region D (see your map of Norland). Irrigation makes it possible to produce either two units of felp or two units of bort on each square of land in Region D. Production in the other regions stays as it was. These amounts and the size of each region are shown in Table A. Use this information to complete Parts 1 through 5.

Table A. Region Production and Size

	1. Number of Squares of Land	2. Units of Bort per Square of Land	3. Units of Felp per Square of Land
Region A	10	2	4
Region B	20	6	2
Region C	10	4	1
Region D	10	2	2

PART 1
Determine the opportunity cost of producing one unit of felp in each region.
    Region A: _____ unit(s) of bort
    Region B: _____ unit(s) of bort
    Region C: _____ unit(s) of bort
    Region D: _____ unit(s) of bort

PART 2
Given your answers in Part 1, determine the order in which these regions should be used for felp production in order to have the smallest reduction in the amount of bort produced.
    First region: _____
    Second region: _____
    Third region: _____
    Last region: _____

ACTIVITY 2.3 (continued)
ASSESSMENT

PART 3

Given your answers in Parts 1 and 2, complete Table B to show the maximum amount of bort Norland could produce given the amounts of felp shown.

Table B. New Production Possibilities for Norland

	1.	2.	3.	4.	5.	6.	7.	8.	9.	10.	11.	12.
Units of felp	0	10	20	30	40	50	60	70	80	90	100	110
Units of bort												

PART 4

For the combination in Column 7, identify the regions in which Norland must produce felp and bort to achieve 60 units of felp and 160 units of bort.

PART 5

Why should people consider opportunity cost when making production decisions?

Lesson 3 - Economics and Population Demographics

OVERVIEW

In this lesson, the students use data and graphs to analyze and compare the populations and standards of living for different countries. The students begin by building a population pyramid of the children in their families over three generations. They then analyze population pyramids to describe the demographic structure of different countries' populations and to analyze the implications of these data. Studying spider graphs, the students learn about the education and health of the populations of different countries and the linkages among investment in human capital, productivity and increased standards of living.

Geography: Geographers use population pyramids to describe the characteristics and distribution of human populations on the earth's surface. They also use these data to analyze social and economic issues to predict future problems that will need to be addressed. For example, a large population of children – ages 0 to 15 years old – will require more schools and teachers today and in the future. A large aging population of people – 50 years and older – suggests a rising current and future demand for medical care and retirement facilities.

Economics: Like geographers, economists are concerned about the impact that different population groups could have on the economy and specifically the demand for goods and services. Economists are also interested in the standard of living for people throughout the world. Living standards are directly related to labor productivity, and an important factor in increasing productivity is a healthy and well-educated labor force. If a country does not invest in its human capital, its labor productivity, as measured by per capita GDP, will remain stagnant or even decrease.

CONCEPTS

Geography
Demographer
Population pyramid
Infant mortality
Life expectancy
Literacy rate
Average years of schooling completed

Economics
Gross domestic product
Gross domestic product per capita
Standard of living
Labor productivity
Human capital
Intermediate goods

CONTENT STANDARDS

Geography
1. How to use maps and other geographic representations, tools and technologies to acquire, process and report information from a spatial perspective

9. The characteristics, distribution and migration of human populations on Earth's surface

Economics
15. Growth: Investment in factories, machinery, new technology, and in the health, education, and training of people can raise future standards of living.

18. Circular Flow and Interdependence: A nation's overall levels of income, employment, and prices are determined by the interaction of spending and production decisions made by all households, firms, government agencies, and others in the economy.

OBJECTIVES

The students will:

1. Use population pyramids to describe the demographic structure of a population.

2. Make predictions based on analysis of specific age groups and describe the implications of these predictions.

3. Explain the relationship between productivity and gross domestic product (GDP) per capita.

4. Explain the relationship between a well-educated and healthy population and a country's standard of living.

5. Define labor productivity, standard of living and human capital.

TIME REQUIRED

70 minutes (**NOTE:** The students must complete one homework assignment before they can do this lesson. See Activity 3.1 and the first two steps under Procedure.)

MATERIALS

1. Visuals 3.1, 3.2, 3.3, 3.4, 3.5, 3.6, 3.7, 3.8 (**NOTE:** Visual 3.3 and Activity 3.2 are the same. Visual 3.7 and Activity 3.4 are the same.)

2. One copy of Activities 3.1, 3.2, 3.3, 3.4 and 3.5 for each student

3. Transparency pen

PROCEDURE

1. Tell the students that this activity will help them use data and graphs to analyze and compare the populations and standards of living for different countries.

2. Distribute a copy of Activity 3.1 to each student. Explain that the class is going to gather information on the number of children in their household and in the households of their parents and grand-

parents when they were children. The class will tally the information and make a bar graph. Tell the students to complete Activity 3.1 with an adult in their families. Assign a date for them to bring the completed activity to class, and tell them to write this date on the appropriate line of the activity.

3. On the day when the students bring their completed activity to class, display Visual 3.1. On the visual, tally the number of male children and female children in the students' households. Do the same for the number of children in the households of their parents and grandparents.

4. Demonstrate how to convert data into a bar graph using the sample on Visual 3.2. The data for "Children in students' households" has been completed. Point out that the bar to the left of center is for males and the bar to the right is for females. Show the students how to complete the data for the other two categories.

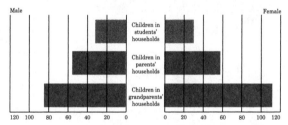

5. Again using Visual 3.2, discuss the following questions to be sure the students can read the graph:

    A. Does the graph show increasing or decreasing household population? Explain. *Decreasing. The population of households decreased. During the past century in the United States, the number of people living in households has decreased with each new generation, although the population of the country has continued to rise.*

    B. In which age group was the male population greater than the female? *Children in students' households*

6. Distribute a copy of Activity 3.2 to each student and display Visual 3.1. Instruct the students to complete the graph with the information for their households using the data from the visual. As the students work, complete the graph on Visual 3.3.

7. Display the completed graph on Visual 3.3, and have the students check their graphs.

8. Discuss the following questions:
    A. What has happened to the size of their households during three generations? *Answers may vary, but most likely the size has decreased.*
    B. Which generation had the most male children? The least? *Answers will vary.*
    C. What do you predict will happen to the size of households in the next generation? Explain. *Answers will vary.*

9. Tell the students that when they collected and analyzed family data, they were **demographers.** Explain that demographers are people who study how population is distributed spatially and by gender, age, occupation and other indicators.

10. Explain that one way demographers analyze data is through the use of **population pyramids**. Tell the students that a population pyramid is a bar graph showing the distribution by gender and age of a region or country's population. A population pyramid shows the percentage or number of total population in five-year age groups. The length of the bar represents the total population in the group; males are on the left, females on the right.

11. Point out that the graph the students made had population distribution by gender but not by age. Display Visual 3.4. Tell the students that this is a population pyramid for Afghanistan. It includes both the age and gender of the country's population. Ask the following questions to be sure the students understand how to read a population pyramid:

    A. On which part of the pyramid is most of the population located? *At the base*
    B. What age groups are represented on this part of the pyramid? *Younger people*
    C. With this population distribution, what issues would the government of this country be concerned about? *Schools, employment, housing*
    D. What goods and services might be in demand? *Answers might include day-care centers, recreation facilities and educators.*

12. Explain that geographers use population pyramids to describe the characteristics and distribution of human populations on the Earth's surface. Economists use them to determine which goods and services the population will produce and consume.

13. Tell the students that they are now going to analyze population pyramids for six different countries.

14. Divide the students into five groups. Distribute a copy of Activity 3.3 to each student. Ask the students to work with their group members to study the population pyramids and answer the questions. After the students have completed their work, review the answers.
    A. Explain the shape of the pyramids, highlighting major differences such as more males than females in certain age groups and bulges in specific sections. *Answers will vary and include the following: Mexico and Kenya have much younger populations than the other countries and fewer people in the older age groups. Germany and the United States have a population bulge in the age groups between 30 and 49. Japan has population bulges in the 25 to 34 age group and for people in their 50s. The United States, Italy, Germany and Japan have substantially more women than men in the oldest age groups.*

B. With this population distribution, what are some major issues that these countries might need to address? *Countries with older populations typically are concerned about a work force large enough to provide goods and services as the population ages and the ability to supply goods and services such as hospitals, retirement homes and retirement funds for older citizens. Countries with younger populations typically are concerned about entry-level jobs and training, housing, education, infrastructure and recreational facilities.*

C. What goods and services might be in demand? *The types of goods and services demanded reflect the needs of the larger age groups; for example, a country with a predominately young population would have a greater demand for teachers, schools, child care, amusement parks, new or expanding businesses to provide jobs.*

15. Tell the students that population pyramids provide a great deal of information about the size and distribution of a country's population, but they don't give information about either the quality of life or the **standard of living** of the people in that country. Explain that standard of living is a measure of the material well-being of a country's citizens. It is often measured as **gross domestic product per capita**.

16. Define **gross domestic product** as the total market value of all final goods and services produced in the economy in one year.

17. Explain that **intermediate goods** are goods used in the production of other goods and services. Intermediate goods are not counted as part of GDP to avoid double counting. For example, if a bakery buys 2,000 pounds of flour to produce pies, cakes and bread, the flour isn't counted as part of GDP. The flour in this example is an intermediate good. The pies, cakes and

bread are final goods that are counted in GDP.

18. Explain that **per capita** means per person. Per capita GDP means how much of the GDP – goods and services – is available for each person in a country. Per capita GDP is determined by dividing the country's total GDP by its population.

19. Divide the class into two uneven groups, one with two-thirds of the students and one with the remainder. Tell the students that the larger group represents Country A and the smaller group is Country B. Write $200 on the board. Tell the countries they each have an identical GDP of $200.

20. Ask the students to determine the per capita GDP for their country. *The country with the smaller population will have a higher per capita GDP.*

21. Discuss the following:
    A. What must either country do to improve its standard of living? *Increase its per capita GDP*
    B. How might they do this? *Increase the number of goods and services they produce, promote slower growth in population or a combination of both*

22. Explain that throughout the world, living standards are directly related to **labor productivity**. Labor productivity is the amount of output per worker. Increasing labor productivity means that each worker produces more output. One way a nation can increase its GDP and its per capita GDP is to improve the skills and knowledge of its labor force. Point out that countries with higher standards of living – higher per capita GDP – have workers who are healthier and better educated and have populations that are growing at a slower rate than countries with lower standards of living.

23. Explain that in addition to looking at the distribution of a country's population

using population pyramids, geographers and economists are also concerned about evaluating a country's **human capital**. Human capital is the quality of labor resources, which a country can improve by making investments in education, training and health.

24. Explain that one way to measure the level of human capital in a country is to look at data related to the population's health and education. These data include **infant mortality rate, life expectancy, literacy rate** and **average years of schooling completed.** Display Visual 3.5 and define the four indicators.

25. Display Visual 3.6 and explain that the diagram is a **spider graph**. Spider graphs are a way of representing data by plotting points on a grid with a number of axes, each with its own scale. Drawing lines from a data point on one axis to the data points on the other axes creates a shape that shows a relationship among the data. This graph shows the infant mortality rate, life expectancy, average years of schooling completed and literacy rate for Afghanistan. Discuss the following:

    A. What does this graph tell us about the health of this country's people? *Low life expectancy and high infant mortality rate indicate that the health of the citizens is poor.*

    B. What does this graph tell us about the education of the people? *Citizens are poorly educated. They have a low literacy rate and spend few years in formal schooling.*

26. Have the students work in the same groups as assigned earlier. Distribute a copy of Activity 3.4 to each group. Instruct the students to answer the questions.

27. When the students have completed the work, display Visual 3.7. Discuss the following questions:

    A. Which countries' spider graphs have similar shapes? *U.S., Japan, Germany*

and Italy have similar shapes because they all have relatively high literacy rates, high average number of years of schooling completed, low infant mortality rates and high life expectancy. Mexico and Kenya are similar because they both have relatively high infant mortality rates, low life expectancy, low literacy rates and low average years of schooling completed.

    B. What generalization can you make from the data? *Countries with better-educated and healthier populations tend to have low infant mortality rates and longer life expectancy.*

    C. What impact might this have on a country's standard of living? *Living standards throughout the world are directly related to labor productivity – producing more per worker. Workers who are healthy, skilled and educated generally are more productive.*

    D. How would a healthier, better-educated population affect a country's per capita GDP? *A healthier, better-educated population would increase per capita GDP, other things being equal.*

28. Display the top of Visual 3.8 (hide the two tables). Tell the students they are going to play a matching game. You are going to give them five minutes to match the per capita GDP to the appropriate country. The group with the most correct answers gets extra credit points (or some other small reward). Tell the groups to use the population and economic data they analyzed on the countries' population pyramids and spider graphs to help them. At the end of five minutes, ask each group to give you their answers. Record the answers on Table A. Ask the students to discuss the reasons why they ranked the countries as they did. *Answers will vary, but they should be able to explain that countries with higher per capita GDP have a well-educated and healthy labor force. Countries with higher infant mortality rates and lower life expectancy will have less-produc-*

tive workers and a lower per capita GDP. Show the students Table B, with the answers. Give the winning group a round of applause.

CLOSURE

29. Use the following questions to review the key points of the lesson:

A. What is a demographer? *A person who looks at how population is distributed spatially and by gender, age, occupation and other indicators*

B. What is a population pyramid? *A population pyramid is a bar graph that shows the distribution by gender and age of a country's population.*

C. What predictions can you make from analyzing the population pyramid? *A large population of youth will likely require more schools, housing and future job opportunities. A relatively large population aged 50 to 65 years old reflects a maturing population, which could create a demand for medical and retirement facilities.*

D. What is gross domestic product and gross domestic product per capita? *The total market value of all final goods and services produced in an economy in a year. Per capita GDP is a country's gross domestic product divided by its population.*

E. How can countries improve their standard of living? *Increase their per capita GDP*

F. How might a country do this? *Increase the number of goods and services it produces, promote slower growth in population or a combination of both*

G. What is one factor that will determine whether a country is able to increase its per capita GDP? *Answers will vary and include better-trained workers, healthy workers, slowing birth rate.*

H. What is human capital? *The quality of labor resources, which a country can improve by making investments in education, training and health*

I. What are some statistics that indicate the level of human capital in a country? *Infant mortality rate, life expectancy, average years of schooling completed and literacy rate*

ASSESSMENT

Distribute a copy of Activity 3.5 to each student. Review the instructions with the students.

Egypt: Egypt has a relatively large number of young people in its population. This means it may face problems providing adequate health care, education and other services for children and parents. The average number of years of schooling is fewer than six, and less than 60% of Egypt's population is literate. A relatively high proportion of babies die before reaching the age of 1, but life expectancy is more than 60 years. Egypt could have trouble attracting businesses that want a well-educated labor force, and this could lower the standard of living and cause some young people to move to other countries to find work.

France: France's population is relatively evenly distributed, with more middle-aged people than young people. The country also has a relatively high number of very old women (over the age of 80). France will face a need for greater geriatric health-care as citizens aged 30 to 54 grow older, particularly because life expectancy is long (averaging almost 80 years). The infant mortality rate is low (fewer than five babies in 1,000 die before their first birthday). Even though the French average only about eight years of schooling, virtually everyone can read and write. France should have a relatively high standard of living because of its healthy and literate labor force.

VISUAL 3.1
CLASS POPULATION STATISTICS

Total number of children in the students' households	
Number of sisters	
Number of brothers	
Total number of children in the parents' households	
Number of sisters	
Number of brothers	
Total number of children in the grandparents' households	
Number of sisters	
Number of brothers	

VISUAL 3.2
CONVERTING DATA INTO A BAR GRAPH

Sample Class Population Statistics

	Number of Brothers	**Number of Sisters**
Children in students' households	32	30
Children in parents' households	55	58
Children in grandparents' households	84	112

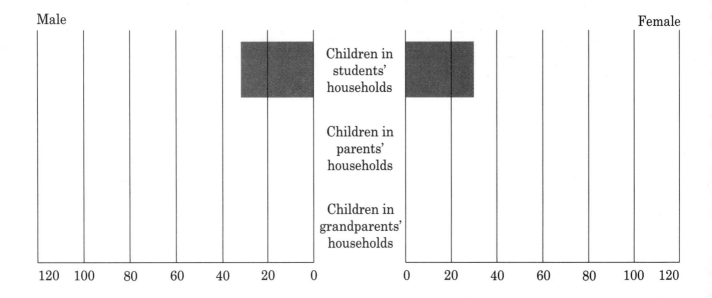

VISUAL 3.3
CLASS BAR GRAPH

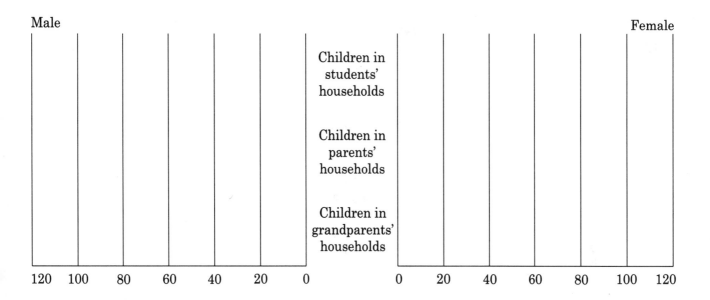

VISUAL 3.4
POPULATION PYRAMID FOR AFGHANISTAN

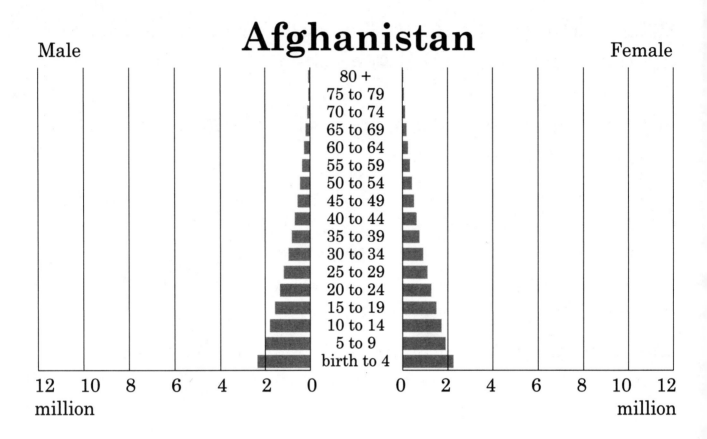

Source for all population pyramids: U.S. Bureau of the Census, International Database, 2003

VISUAL 3.5
INDICATORS

Infant Mortality Rate: the number of babies who die out of every 1,000 live births

Life Expectancy: the number of years an individual is expected to live at birth

Literacy Rate: the percentage of people over 15 years of age who can read and write

Average Years of Schooling Completed: the average years of schooling that adults over the age of 15 receive

VISUAL 3.6
SPIDER GRAPH FOR AFGHANISTAN

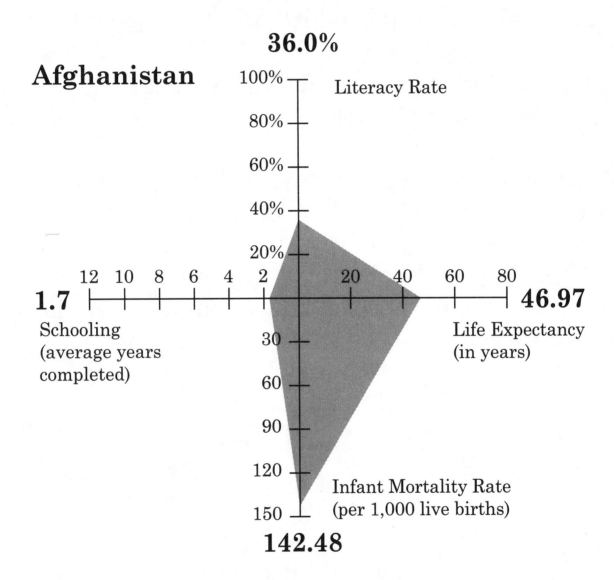

36.0%

Afghanistan

100% — Literacy Rate

80%

60%

40%

20%

12 10 8 6 4 2   20   40   60   80

1.7   **46.97**

Schooling
(average years
completed)

30   Life Expectancy
(in years)

60

90

120 Infant Mortality Rate
150 (per 1,000 live births)

142.48

Sources for all spider graphs: The World Factbook, Central Intelligence Agency, 2003,
and The World Bank Group; most recent data available

VISUAL 3.7
SPIDER GRAPHS

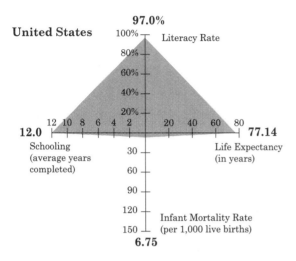

United States
97.0% Literacy Rate
Schooling (average years completed) 12.0
Life Expectancy (in years) 77.14
Infant Mortality Rate (per 1,000 live births) 6.75

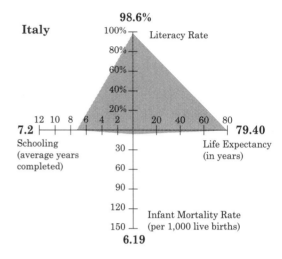

Italy
98.6% Literacy Rate
Schooling (average years completed) 7.2
Life Expectancy (in years) 79.40
Infant Mortality Rate (per 1,000 live births) 6.19

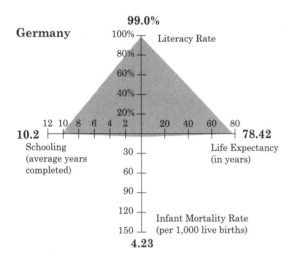

Germany
99.0% Literacy Rate
Schooling (average years completed) 10.2
Life Expectancy (in years) 78.42
Infant Mortality Rate (per 1,000 live births) 4.23

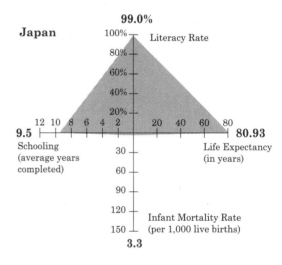

Japan
99.0% Literacy Rate
Schooling (average years completed) 9.5
Life Expectancy (in years) 80.93
Infant Mortality Rate (per 1,000 live births) 3.3

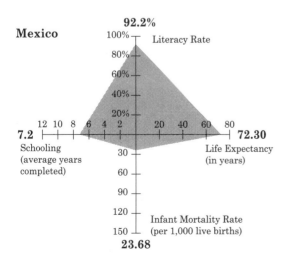

Mexico
92.2% Literacy Rate
Schooling (average years completed) 7.2
Life Expectancy (in years) 72.30
Infant Mortality Rate (per 1,000 live births) 23.68

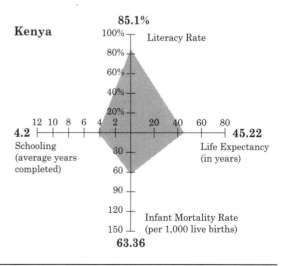

Kenya
85.1% Literacy Rate
Schooling (average years completed) 4.2
Life Expectancy (in years) 45.22
Infant Mortality Rate (per 1,000 live births) 63.36

VISUAL 3.8
MATCHING GAME

Match the country with the correct per capita GDP.

Country	Per Capita GDP
Afghanistan	$700
Germany	$1,100
Italy	$8,900
Kenya	$25,100
Mexico	$26,200
Japan	$28,700
United States	$36,300

Table A. Matching

Country	Group 1	Group 2	Group 3	Group 4	Group 5
Afghanistan					
Germany					
Italy					
Kenya					
Mexico					
Japan					
United States					

Table B. Answers

Country	Per Capita GDP
Afghanistan	*$700*
Germany	*$26,200*
Italy	*$25,100*
Kenya	*$1,100*
Mexico	*$8,900*
Japan	*$28,700*
United States	*$36,300*

Source: The CIA World Factbook

ACTIVITY 3.1
DATA COLLECTION

Return to class by _____

As part of our study of population statistics, you are going to gather data about the size of your household. Interview an adult relative to learn the number of children in one parent's and one grandparent's households. Record the information in the chart below.

Family population statistics for _____ family

(Your name)

Total number of children in my household	
Number of sisters	
Number of brothers	
Total number of children in my parent's household	
Number of sisters	
Number of brothers	
Total number of children in my grandparent's household	
Number of sisters	
Number of brothers	

ACTIVITY 3.2
CLASS BAR GRAPH

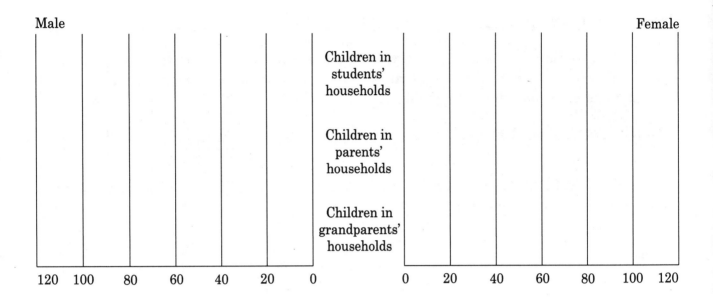

Male

Female

Children in
students'
households

Children in
parents'
households

Children in
grandparents'
households

120   100   80   60   40   20   0   0   20   40   60   80   100   120

ACTIVITY 3.3
POPULATION PYRAMIDS

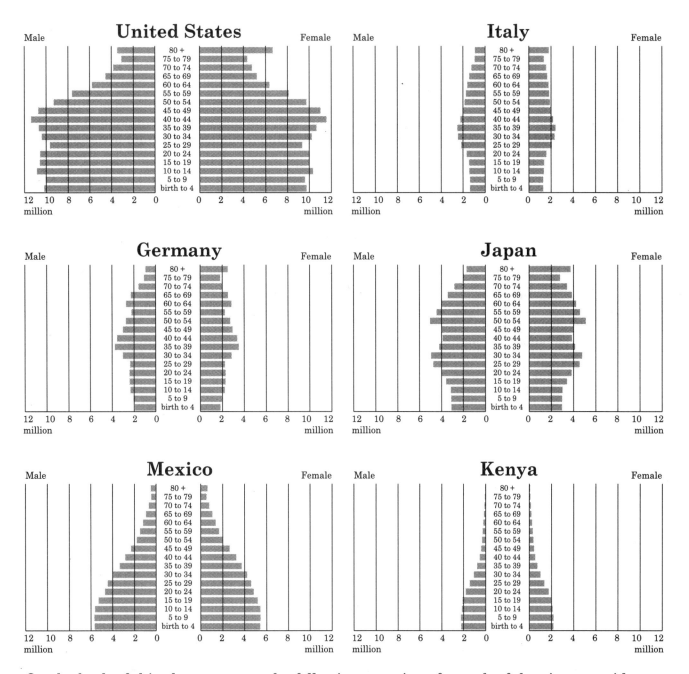

On the back of this sheet, answer the following questions for each of the six pyramids.

A. Explain the shape of the pyramid, highlighting major differences such as more males than females in certain age groups and bulges in specific sections.

B. With this population distribution, what are some major problems that this country might need to address?

C. What goods and services might be in demand?

ACTIVITY 3.4
SPIDER GRAPHS

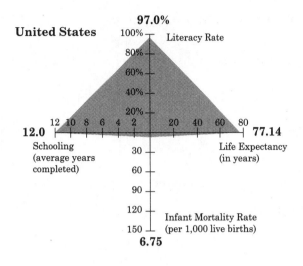

United States

97.0% Literacy Rate

12.0 Schooling (average years completed)

77.14 Life Expectancy (in years)

6.75 Infant Mortality Rate (per 1,000 live births)

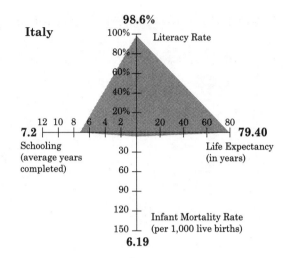

Italy

98.6% Literacy Rate

7.2 Schooling (average years completed)

79.40 Life Expectancy (in years)

6.19 Infant Mortality Rate (per 1,000 live births)

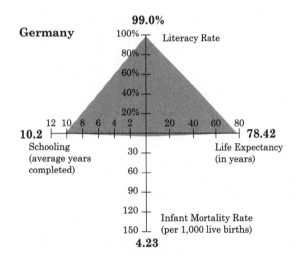

Germany

99.0% Literacy Rate

10.2 Schooling (average years completed)

78.42 Life Expectancy (in years)

4.23 Infant Mortality Rate (per 1,000 live births)

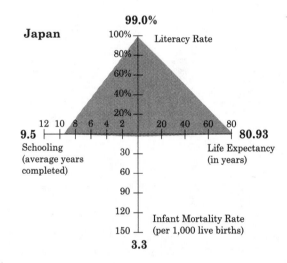

Japan

99.0% Literacy Rate

9.5 Schooling (average years completed)

80.93 Life Expectancy (in years)

3.3 Infant Mortality Rate (per 1,000 live births)

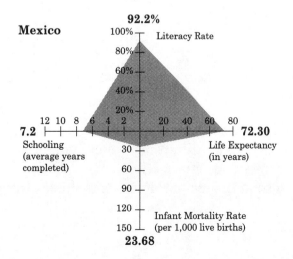

Mexico

92.2% Literacy Rate

7.2 Schooling (average years completed)

72.30 Life Expectancy (in years)

23.68 Infant Mortality Rate (per 1,000 live births)

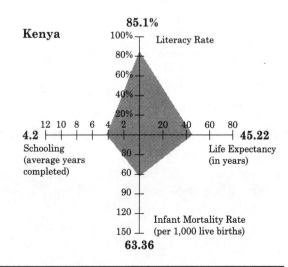

Kenya

85.1% Literacy Rate

4.2 Schooling (average years completed)

45.22 Life Expectancy (in years)

63.36 Infant Mortality Rate (per 1,000 live births)

ACTIVITY 3.4 (continued)
SPIDER GRAPHS

Answer the following questions for each spider graph on the previous page.

1. What does the graph tell us about the health of the country's people?

2. What does it tell us about the education of the people?

3. What do the data tell us about the quality of the country's human (labor) resources?

4. What effect can the level of literacy, education, and health have on a country's GDP?

5. How would this affect a country's per capita GDP if its population is stable?

ACTIVITY 3.5
ASSESSMENT

You are a CIA agent. You have been asked to analyze population and economic data for a country and prepare a report for the president of the United States. Select Egypt or France, and write one or two paragraphs using data from the population pyramid and spider chart to describe the characteristics of your country's people and its standard of living. In your report:
- Describe the country's population distribution.
- Identify potential problems the country may face because of its population distribution and explain why.
- Describe the health and education of the population.
- Explain the impact these conditions will have on the country's standard of living and why.

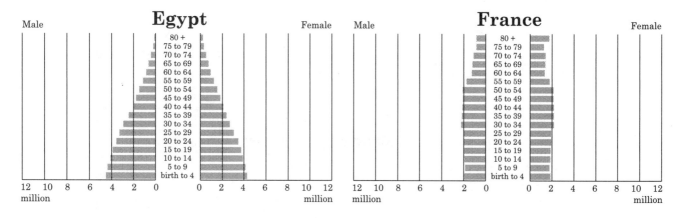

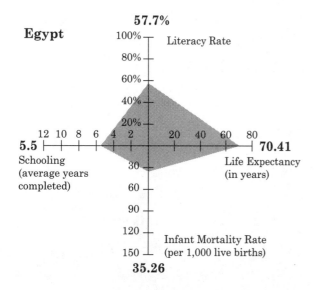

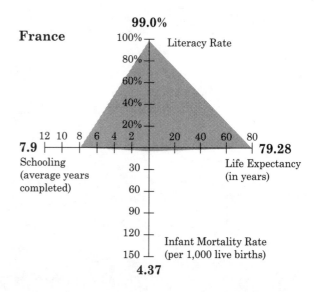

Lesson 4 - Why Do People Move?

OVERVIEW

In this lesson, the students learn that costs and benefits influence people's decisions about moving. The students review U.S. Census data to discuss possible reasons why people move. They analyze the costs and benefits of moving. They are introduced to the geographic terms push and pull factors of migration. Working in groups, the students read about a family that chooses to migrate to another country. The students identify costs and benefits for the family and then determine whether push or pull factors had the greatest influence. Finally, the students look at some current data about migration to the United States.

Geography: Geographers study the forces behind the movement of people from one location to another. Some moves are voluntary, involving the search for a higher standard of living or elevation of status through jobs or education. Some of these moves are involuntary, caused by war, natural disasters and economic or political upheaval. Geographic literacy requires the students to understand the push and pull factors that lead to migration and what influences people to migrate from one place to another.

Economics: Because of unlimited wants and limited resources, people must make decisions. Economists study the factors that influence the decisions people make. By studying the costs and benefits of alternatives people have, economists hope to better understand the decision-making process. As with any decision, people analyze the costs and benefits of alternatives before making a decision to migrate.

CONCEPTS

Geography
  Migration
  Immigrants
  Pull Factors
  Push Factors

Economics
  Costs
  Benefits
  Decision making

CONTENT STANDARDS

Geography
9. The characteristics, distribution and migration of human populations on Earth's surface

12. The process, patterns and functions of human settlement

13. How forces of cooperation and conflict among people influence the division and control of Earth's surface

Economics
2. Marginal Cost/Marginal Benefit: Effective decision making requires comparing the additional costs of alternatives with the additional benefits.

4. Role of Incentives: People respond predictably to positive and negative incentives.

OBJECTIVES

The students will:
1. Read census tables and graphs to obtain information and draw conclusions.

2. Define costs and benefits, and identify the costs and benefits that influence people's decisions to migrate.

3. Define push and pull factors for migration, and identify examples.

TIME REQUIRED

60 minutes

MATERIALS

1. Visuals 4.1 and 4.2 (**NOTE:** Visual 4.2 and Activity 4.3 are the same.)

2. Activity 4.1 cut apart to provide a card for each group

3. One copy of Activity 4.2 for each group

4. One copy of Activities 4.3, 4.4 and 4.5 for each student

PROCEDURE

1. Ask the students to raise their hand if they have ever moved. Ask for volunteers to share the distance or number of times they have moved. Share a personal moving story if the students do not volunteer enough examples. Tell the students that in this lesson, they will analyze why people move.

2. Display Visual 4.1. Draw attention to Figure 1. If the students have reported recent moves, ask them to select the category they think they fall into. *Answers will vary from same county, different county same state, different state and movers from abroad.* Point out that more than half the moves are within the same county. Have the students speculate why most people move within the same county. *Answers will vary; most may move for better housing, schools, employment or similar reasons.*

3. Direct the students to look at Figure 2. Discuss the following questions:
    A. Which age group moves the most, according to this chart? *Ages 20 to 24*
    B. Why do you think this group moves the most? *Answers should reflect that*

this age group usually has the most life-changing events such as graduation, new job, marriage, childbirth, fewer family or job ties to a location.
    C. Why do you think the oldest group, 85+, has such a low rate for moving? *Answers will vary and include more ties to the community, family and friends that might make moves more difficult; less income since this age group is likely to be retired; usually space needs are decreasing rather than increasing; health issues.*

4. Direct the students to Figure 3. Have the students locate the region in the United States where they live. Point out that **migration** is the act of moving from one place to another with the intent of staying permanently or for a relatively long period of time, and people who move into an area are called **immigrants**.

5. Tell the students to use Figure 3 to determine where most new immigrants to their region came from and then discuss Questions A and B. *The highest number of migrants moving into Northeastern, Midwestern and Western states came from Southern states. The highest number of migrants moving into the South came from the Midwest.*
    A. Have you met anyone who recently moved from one of these regions? *Answers will vary.*
    B. Why did the person or family move here? *Answers will vary.*

6. Explain that **benefits** and **costs** influence the decisions people make. Benefits are the advantages of a particular course of action as measured by good feelings, dollars or number of items. Costs are the disadvantages of a particular course of action as measured by bad feelings, dollars or numbers of items. Point out that costs and benefits may be different for different people. Use the following scenario to clarify the meaning of costs and benefits:
    Suppose you are deciding what to do

with three hours of after-school time. You could spend this time listening to music or baby-sitting for a neighbor. The neighbor will pay $4.00 an hour and really needs your help because she must visit a sick family member. However, her children are unruly and sometimes don't listen to you when you stay with them.

7. Make two columns on the board, with "Costs" at the top of one and "Benefits" at the top of the other. Ask the students to identify the costs and benefits from the scenario. Write each in the appropriate column, and discuss the students' answers. *Answers will vary and include the desire for extra money and good feelings as benefits and unruly children and the low wage as costs.* **NOTE:** The students may disagree about costs and benefits. Some may say that taking care of small children is a benefit because they really enjoy being with young children. Others may say it is a cost because they consider it hard work. If there is disagreement, tell the students that costs and benefits may differ because of different values, likes and dislikes.

8. Ask how many of the students might be willing to baby-sit and why. *Answers will vary.* Explain that different students will respond differently to these costs and benefits, based on their financial needs or their enjoyment from spending after-school time baby-sitting.

9. Tell the students that they are going to apply the concepts of costs and benefits to the examples they have been looking at for region-to-region migrations.

10. As a class, brainstorm a list of costs and benefits that would influence people's decisions to move from one area to another. *Answers will vary. Benefits may include new or better job, better weather, friends currently living in the new location, lower taxes, beautiful environment, recreational*

opportunities. Costs may include the expense of moving, climate, lack of jobs, crowded conditions, high taxes. Remind the students that what constitutes a cost or benefit differs depending on the values, likes and dislikes of different people. Cold weather might be a benefit for a skier and a cost for an elderly couple.

11. Explain that many factors influence people's decisions to migrate voluntarily. Discuss the following:
    • People who earn lower wages are more likely to migrate if they believe they will earn higher wages after migrating. They perceive the future benefits as greater than the current costs.
    • People who earn higher wages and live in countries with very high tax rates are more likely to migrate to reduce their tax burden. They perceive the future benefits as greater than the current costs.
    • People who speak the language of the country to which they migrate are more likely to migrate because their current costs (learning a new language) are lower.
    • People who are able to move to countries where they have friends or family – or where there is a large community of others from their home country – are more likely to migrate because they have lower current costs.
    • Younger people are more likely to migrate because the future benefits are greater: They will have a better job, more income and better living conditions for a longer period of time than people who migrate when they are older.
    • People who value future income more than current income are more likely to migrate. They place greater value on future benefits than on current costs.
    • People who are less adverse to risk are more likely to migrate.
    Point out that in cases such as war, famine and genocide, a great number of people will likely move. Migration is no longer voluntary.

12. Tell the students that geographers study migration, or moving patterns of groups of people, to discover why people have moved. Local officials can use this information to plan for increases or decreases in population to various areas so they can provide services, housing, job training or tax incentives to the new migrant groups.

13. Explain that geographers group reasons for migration into two categories: **push factors** that drive people to move away from an area and **pull factors** that draw people to a certain location. Ask the students for examples of pull factors (*nice weather, location of relatives*) and push factors (*closing of factory, drought*) to make sure they understand the differences among push factors, pull factors, costs and benefits. Discuss the following:

   A. What are benefits? *Benefits are the advantages of a particular course of action as measured by good feelings, dollars or number of items.*

   B. What are costs? *Costs are the disadvantages of a particular course of action as measured by bad feelings, dollars or numbers of items.*

   C. Are push factors costs or benefits? Why? *Costs, because they are disadvantages of a location that would drive people to move away*
(**NOTE**: Make sure the students understand that the costs of moving to a new location are not push factors; for example, having to learn a new language when you move to a new country is a cost of moving, but it isn't a push factor because it isn't a disadvantage of your original location that drove you to move away.)

   D. Are pull factors costs or benefits? Why? *Benefits, because they are advantages that would draw people to move to a particular location.*
(**NOTE**: Make sure the students understand that the benefits of staying in a location are not pull factors: Not changing schools is a benefit of staying in your neighborhood; it isn't an advantage that would draw you to a new location.)

14. Tell the students that in 2002 the United Nations estimated that around 175 million people, or about 3 percent of the world's population, resided in a country different from their country of birth. Explain that the students will work in groups to learn more about reasons for migration. Divide the students into six groups. Distribute one card from Activity 4.1 and a copy of Activity 4.2 to each group. Review the directions for Part 1 with the class.

15. Draw two columns on the board. Label one column "Push Factors for Migration" and the other "Pull Factors for Migration." Have the students read their cards and complete Part 1 of Activity 4.2. When the groups are finished, have them share their information with the rest of the class. As the groups share, record examples of push and pull factors in the appropriate columns on the board. Remind the students that push factors are costs because they represent disadvantages of staying in the current location and pull factors are benefits because they represent advantages of moving to a new location. *Push factors: Andre, persecution; Thomas, shortage of land; Alejandro, revolution; Nguyen, war; Naomi, persecution; Yuri, shortage of food and jobs. Pull factors: Andre, acceptance; Thomas, available land; Nguyen, freedom; Naomi, work, respect and education; Yuri, employment and education*

16. Review the bulleted items from No. 11 on the previous page. Have the students work in the same groups as for the previous activity. Review the questions for Part 2 of Activity 4.2. Allow time for the students to finish Part 2. Have a member from each group share answers with the class. *Question A
Andre: Benefits are acceptance, possible work, education for Andre, friends already there. Costs are leaving possessions, family and friends; perhaps having to learn a new language and new customs; difficult travel*

Nguyen: Benefits are freedom, possibility of work, education for Nguyen. Costs are leaving friends and possessions, learning a new language, learning new customs, cost of travel.
Thomas: Benefits are possibility of owing land, access to food. Costs are giving up possessions, leaving family and friends.
Naomi: Benefits are freedom, possibility of work, respect, education for children, family member already there. Costs are leaving relatives and friends, learning a new language and new customs, giving up possessions
Alejandro: Benefits are safety, possibility of finding work. Costs are giving up possessions, learning a new language and customs.
Yuri: Benefits are possibility of work, friends already there, education for Yuri. Costs are leaving behind friends and family, transportation, possibly learning a new language, learning new customs.
Question B: Answers will vary.

17. Display Visual 4.2 and give each student a copy of Activity 4.3. Tell the students that the immigration data were collected by the U.S. Department of Homeland Security's Office of Immigration Statistics based on the major legal-status categories available to migrants who apply to enter the United States. These categories include sponsorship by a relative, requests for asylum or refuge from people who want to avoid persecution in their home countries and employment-based preferences (preferences given to people with skills that are in demand in the United States). Ask the students if they think these legal-status categories reflect all – or even the main – reasons why people migrate to the United States. *Answers will vary, but most students will probably say no.* Discuss the following questions:

    A. From which country on the map did the largest number of people migrate to the United States in fiscal 2002? *Mexico,*

with 219,380 immigrants

    B. Under what legal-status category did the majority of these people apply to enter the United States? *95% were immediate relatives of U.S. citizens or were sponsored by their family.*

    C. Mexico's per capita (per person) gross domestic product in 2003 was $9,000. Per capita GDP for the United States the same year was $37,800. Does this suggest a reason, beyond the legal-status categories, why Mexican citizens want to come to the United States? *Yes, the opportunity to earn more money and have a higher standard of living is also an attraction.*

    D. Do you think these people migrated mainly because of push factors or pull factors? Explain. *Pull factors: They wanted more income, a higher standard of living and to be with their families and relatives.*

18. Give each student a copy of Activity 4.4, and, using Mexico as an example, demonstrate how to complete the table. Point out that the information for the first two columns comes from the map on Activity 4.3. Have the students individually or in pairs select four additional countries and complete the table, and then answer Questions B and C.

19. When the students have finished their work, allow time for them to share their answers with the class.
    A. Using the map and the information on Activity 4.3, select four countries and complete the table for these countries. *Answers will vary based on countries.*
    B. Give three examples of push factors that influence migration from one place to another. *Closing of factories, drought, war*
    C. Give three examples of pull factors that influence migration from one place to another. *Better job opportunities, relatives living in an area, education, more freedom*

CLOSURE

20. Use the following questions to review the key points of the lesson:

   A. Based on this information, what seems to be the primary reason immigrant groups come to the United States? *Job or educational opportunities*

   B. What do you think are benefits of moving to the United States? *Variety and number of job opportunities, freedom of choice of jobs, ability to move freely in the job market, variety of educational opportunities, technical training available at many locations, size of economy, political freedom, joining relatives, a higher standard of living*

   C. Would these benefits be examples of push or pull factors for migration? Why? *Pull factors, because they are advantages that would draw people to move to the United States*

   D. What are costs of moving to the United States? *Leaving family and friends, cost of travel, finding new housing and a new job, learning a new language*

   E. What are some policies that could reduce immigration to the United States? *Policies that increase economic development and raise the standard of living in other countries, policies that impose limits on the number of immigrants the United States will accept*

ASSESSMENT

Distribute a copy of Activity 4.5 to each student. Review the instructions for the activity with the students.

1, 2. Read the following paragraph and use the information to complete the table below.
   . . . Use the table below to help you make your decision. You may add details not included in the information above to support your decision. *Costs of moving to the new city could include losing the opportunity to play soccer at school, having to live in a smaller house and leaving friends. Benefits of moving could be living closer to grandparents, getting a better education and having access to a richer array of cultural, sports and entertainment options. Costs of staying could include losing the opportunity to meet new friends and get a better education. It's also possible that your mother's career could be hurt if she doesn't take the new job. Benefits of staying could include being able to play soccer on the school team and neighborhood leagues and staying close to friends.*

3. For you, which are greater: the costs or the benefits? Explain. *Answers about whether costs are greater than benefits will vary, based on each student's assessment of the situation.*

4. If you moved, would it be a push or pull migration? Explain. *Answers about whether it would be a push or pull migration will vary. Pull factors will vary and include the allure of living in a new city with new friends and new entertainment options. Push factors also will vary and include lower quality schools.*

VISUAL 4.1
GEOGRAPHIC MOBILITY
2002 to 2003 data for the population 1 year and older

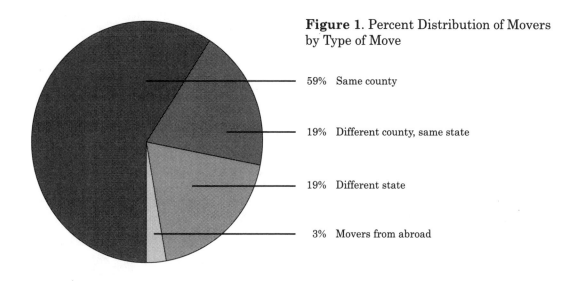

Figure 1. Percent Distribution of Movers by Type of Move

59%   Same county

19%   Different county, same state

19%   Different state

3%   Movers from abroad

Figure 2. Moving Rates by Age

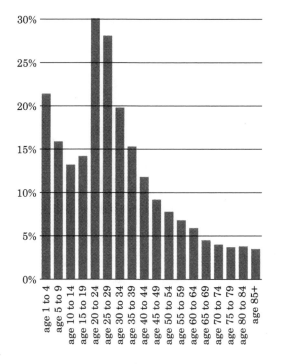

Figure 3. Migration by Region
(in thousands, 2003)

		People moving in (inmigrants)				
		Total	Northeast	Midwest	South	West
	Total	**2,693**	**385**	**574**	**1,016**	**718**
People moving out (outmigrants)	Northeast	**483**	*	71	319	93
	Midwest	**675**	62	*	378	235
	South	**891**	198	303	*	390
	West	**644**	125	200	319	*

Source: U.S. Census Bureau

VISUAL 4.2
IMMIGRANTS ADMITTED TO THE UNITED STATES
Top 20 countries of birth (FY 2002)

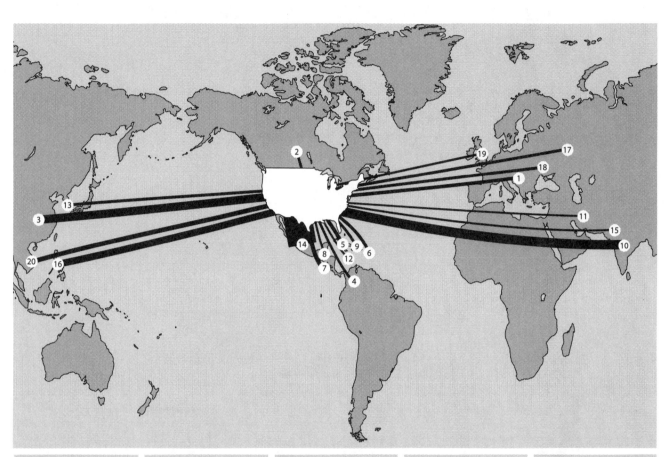

BOSNIA-HERZEGOVINA 25,373 ①	CUBA 28,272 ⑤	HAITI 20,268 ⑨	KOREA, SOUTH 21,021 ⑬	RUSSIA 20,268 ⑰
25,033 were refugees and people seeking asylum	24,893 were refugees and people seeking asylum	6,732 were sponsored by their families	9,573 were immediate relatives of U.S. citizens; 9,241 were admitted on employment-based preferences	10,468 were immediate relatives of U.S. citizens; 5,089 were refugees or seeking asylum
CANADA 19,519 ②	DOMINICAN REPUBLIC 22,604 ⑥	INDIA 71,105 ⑩	MEXICO 219,380 ⑭	UKRAINE 21,217 ⑱
9,530 were admitted on employment-based preferences	6,880 were spouses of U.S. citizens, 2,880 were children of citizens	60% were admitted on employment-based preferences	95% were immediate relatives of U.S. citizens or were sponsored by their family	10,601 were refugees and people seeking asylum
CHINA 61,282 ③	EL SALVADOR 31,168 ⑦	IRAN 13,029 ⑪	PAKISTAN 13,743 ⑮	UNITED KINGDOM 16,181 ⑲
27,911 were children, parents or spouses of U.S. citizens	8,763 were parents, children or spouses of U.S. citizens	4,806 refugees and people seeking asylum were granted permanent resident status	43% were immediate relatives of U.S. citizens; 24% were admitted on employment-based preferences	7,511 were admitted on employment-based preferences; 6,834 were spouses of U.S. citizens
COLOMBIA 18,845 ④	GUATEMALA 16,229 ⑧	JAMAICA 14,898 ⑫	PHILIPPINES 51,308 ⑯	VIETNAM 33,627 ⑳
8,815 were spouses of U.S. citizens; 3,333 were children of citizens	3,579 were spouses of U.S. citizens; 3,468 were children of citizens	96% were immediate relatives of U.S. citizens or were sponsored by their family	26,470 were immediate relatives of U.S. citizens; 12,060 were sponsored by their families	6,926 were refugees or people seeking asylum

Base map by Mapquest

ACTIVITY 4.1
MIGRATION SCENARIOS

Andre – Port-au-Prince, Haiti

It is 1981. Andre and his family live in a village near Port-au-Prince. They do not believe in the policies of Haiti's government, so the government is persecuting them. Andre's family decides to go to America because they know their beliefs will be more accepted there. They have friends there who tell them work is available and Andre can attend school. Andre's family is not wealthy. They cannot travel by airplane because they do not have their government's permission to leave Haiti. They must leave most of their possessions, their friends and many family members behind.

Naomi – Russia

It is 1884. Naomi and her family live in Russia. Her parents have tried running several businesses, but all failed. The government has forced them to live in a restricted area because they are Jews. Naomi's father emigrated to America and has sent money so the family can follow him. In his letters, he tells the family that work is available, workers are treated with respect and all children are allowed to go to school. The family must leave behind many relatives and friends and all but a few of their possessions. Naomi, her mother and siblings do not speak English.

Nguyen – South Vietnam

It is 1975. Nguyen and her family live in a village 20 miles from Saigon. The war between North Vietnam and South Vietnam is almost over. It is a time of terrible hardship. Nguyen's father knows that when the war ends, his family must make many changes he does not want to make. Nguyen's family decides to migrate to America where they will be free. They have heard they will be able to find work and Nguyen can go to school. They are very poor with only a small amount of money to pay for their trip. They leave their few possessions and friends behind.

Alejandro – Central Mexico

It is 1910. Alejandro and his family live in a village in Central Mexico. A great revolution is going on, and it is very dangerous for Alejandro's family. They decide to leave Mexico and travel to America where it is safe and where they will be able to find work. Alejandro's family is very poor; they have only a few possessions that they can barter for transportation to America. They do not speak English, but they have relatives in the United States.

Thomas – Ireland

It is 1890. Thomas and his family live in southern Ireland. Thomas's father wants his own land to farm, but because there is a shortage of good farmland, Thomas's father has to lease land from a landlord. Thomas's family is very poor even though they work hard as farmers. The family hears that America has good farmland, so they decide to emigrate to the Oklahoma Territory. Although they do not have much money, they do have items they can barter for transportation.

Yuri – Ukraine

It is 1995. Yuri and his family live in Ukraine. Ukraine was part of the Soviet Union, but now it is an independent country. Many families struggle to survive because food is scarce. Yuri's father and mother are well educated, but few jobs are available. They decide to emigrate to the United States, to an area where other Ukrainians are living and it is possible to find work. They also know their son can attend school and receive a good education.

ACTIVITY 4.2
WHY FAMILIES MIGRATE

PART 1

Read the card your group was given. Remember there can be a combination of push and pull factors that influence people's decisions to move.

A. List push factors – costs or disadvantages that drive people to move away from a location – for this family.

B. List pull factors – benefits or advantages that draw people to a location – for this family.

PART 2

A. Reread the card your group was given. Make a list of any costs and benefits you can think of for this family in moving to the United States.

B. Would your group have made the same decision as the family on your card? Why?

ACTIVITY 4.3
IMMIGRANTS ADMITTED TO THE UNITED STATES
Top 20 countries of birth (FY 2002)

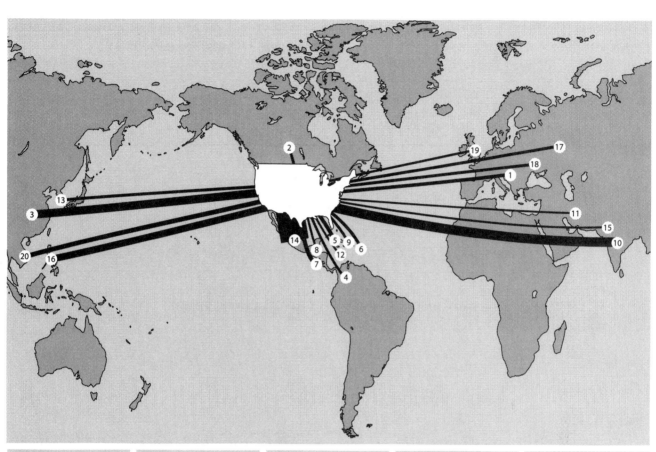

BOSNIA-HERZEGOVINA 25,373 (1)	CUBA 28,272 (5)	HAITI 20,268 (9)	KOREA, SOUTH 21,021 (13)	RUSSIA 20,268 (17)
25,033 were refugees and people seeking asylum	24,893 were refugees and people seeking asylum	6,732 were sponsored by their families	9,573 were immediate relatives of U.S. citizens; 9,241 were admitted on employment-based preferences	10,468 were immediate relatives of U.S. citizens; 5,089 were refugees or seeking asylum
CANADA 19,519 (2)	DOMINICAN REPUBLIC 22,604 (6)	INDIA 71,105 (10)	MEXICO 219,380 (14)	UKRAINE 21,217 (18)
9,530 were admitted on employment-based preferences	6,880 were spouses of U.S. citizens, 2,880 were children of citizens	60% were admitted on employment-based preferences	95% were immediate relatives of U.S. citizens or were sponsored by their family	10,601 were refugees and people seeking asylum
CHINA 61,282 (3)	EL SALVADOR 31,168 (7)	IRAN 13,029 (11)	PAKISTAN 13,743 (15)	UNITED KINGDOM 16,181 (19)
27,911 were children, parents or spouses of U.S. citizens	8,763 were parents, children or spouses of U.S. citizens	4,806 refugees and people seeking asylum were granted permanent resident status	43% were immediate relatives of U.S. citizens; 24% were admitted on employment-based preferences	7,511 were admitted on employment-based preferences; 6,834 were spouses of U.S. citizens
COLOMBIA 18,845 (4)	GUATEMALA 16,229 (8)	JAMAICA 14,898 (12)	PHILIPPINES 51,308 (16)	VIETNAM 33,627 (20)
8,815 were spouses of U.S. citizens; 3,333 were children of citizens	3,579 were spouses of U.S. citizens; 3,468 were children of citizens	96% were immediate relatives of U.S. citizens or were sponsored by their family	26,470 were immediate relatives of U.S. citizens; 12,060 were sponsored by their families	6,926 were refugees or people seeking asylum

Base map by Mapquest

ACTIVITY 4.4
CHART OF PUSH AND PULL FACTORS OF MIGRATION

A. Using the map and the information on Activity 4.3, select four countries and complete the table for these countries. Then answer Questions B and C.

Country from which immigrants are coming to the United States	Number of immigrants coming into the United States	In your group's opinion, is this group of immigrants responding to push or pull factors? Why?

B. Give three examples of push factors that influence migration from one place to another.

C. Give three examples of pull factors that influence migration from one place to another.

ACTIVITY 4.5
ASSESSMENT

1. Read the following paragraph and use the information to complete the table below.

Your parents call a family meeting. Your mother has been offered a new job with a higher salary in a city 1,000 miles away. The new city is bigger than the town you live in now and has many theaters, parks, museums and shopping areas – along with two major-league sports teams. The city is also near the ocean, and you've always wanted to live near the ocean. It has excellent schools and is only half an hour from your favorite grand-parents. You have lived in the same neighborhood all your life, and you and your brother have many friends here. You just made the soccer team at school and had planned to play on a neighborhood team this summer. Your father is a skilled craftsman, and he says he should have no trouble finding jobs in the new city, but it may take him awhile to build up a solid list of clients. So even though your mother will make more money, your family may have to buy a smaller house because home prices are higher in the new city. Your mother says she won't take the new job if the family doesn't want to move, and she asks you how you feel.

2. Use the table below to help you make your decision. You may add details not included in the information above to support your decision.

Alternatives	Costs	Benefits
Move to the new city		
Stay where you now live		

3. For you, which are greater: the costs or the benefits? Explain.

4. If you moved, would it be a push or pull migration? Explain.

Lesson 5 - Economic Freedom: How Important Is It?

OVERVIEW

In this lesson, the students participate in activities that help them understand the correlation between economic freedom and a country's standard of living. First the students decide whether they agree or disagree with rules and laws that affect teenagers. They discuss how rules and laws affect their economic freedom and then hypothesize about how economic freedom affects a country's standard of living and the welfare of its citizens. They hypothesize about the extent of economic freedom in less-developed countries relative to more-developed countries. Using data for a number of economic and geographic indicators, the students test their hypotheses. (**NOTE:** The relationships among data reviewed in this lesson are correlational not causal.)

Geography: Geographers divide countries into two categories according to their level of development:

> • More-developed countries tend to be technologically advanced, highly urbanized and wealthy. A high percentage of their populations are employed in manufacturing and service industries. These countries also tend to have low rates of infant mortality and high literacy rates.
> • Less-developed countries tend to have low rates of urbanization, and a high percentage of their populations are employed in agriculture. They also have high rates of infant mortality and illiteracy.

Geographers ask why development varies among countries. To answer this question they look at data such as gross domestic product, gross domestic product per capita, literacy rates, infant mortality and the three basic ways people earn their living: agriculture, manufacturing goods and providing services.

Economics: Economic systems strive to achieve a set of broad social goals that may include economic freedom, efficiency, equity, growth and stability. How successful an economy is in achieving these goals affects the country's ability to improve its citizens' standards of living. Institutions and policies that promote a stable political and economic climate and that help to encourage economic growth are extremely important. Economic freedom refers to the freedom for consumers to decide how to spend or save their incomes, for workers to change jobs or join unions, for people to establish new businesses or close old ones and similar opportunities for people to make economic decisions. Each year, The Heritage Foundation and The Wall Street Journal publish an Index of Economic Freedom. The index is based on 10 factors: trade policy, the fiscal burden of government (marginal tax rates and changes in government spending as a percentage of gross domestic product), government intervention in the economy (consumption and production), monetary policy, capital flows and foreign investment, banking and finance, wages and prices, property rights, government regulation and the extent of informal or underground market activities. More freedom – less regulation – is correlated with higher levels of income and growth. Higher levels of income and growth, other things equal, lead to higher standards of living and a higher level of welfare for citizens.

CONCEPTS

Geography
> More-developed countries
> Less-developed countries
> Primary, secondary and
>   tertiary economic activity
> Gross domestic product
> Gross domestic product per capita
> Standard of living
> Choropleth map

Economics
Gross domestic product
Gross domestic product per capita
Standard of living
Economic freedom

CONTENT STANDARDS

Geography
7. The physical processes that shape the patterns of Earth's surface

11. The patterns and networks of economic interdependence on Earth's surface

Economics
1. Scarcity: Productive resources are limited. Therefore, people cannot have all the goods and services they want; as a result, they must choose some things and give up others.

15. Growth: Investment in factories, machinery, new technology and the health, education, and training of people can raise future standards of living.

18. Circular Flow/Interdependence: A nation's overall levels of income, employment, and prices are determined by the interaction of spending and production decisions made by all households, firms, government agencies, and others in the economy.

OBJECTIVES

The students will:
1. Define economic freedom, economic growth, gross domestic product, standard of living, more-developed and less-developed countries and primary, secondary and tertiary economic activity.

2. Explain the relationship between a country's level of economic freedom and
   • its standard of living
   • the welfare of its citizens.

3. Explain the relationship between economic freedom and economic development.

TIME REQUIRED

90 minutes

MATERIALS

1. Visuals 5.1, 5.2, 5.3, 5.4 and 5.5 (**NOTE:** Visual 5.4 and Activity 5.1 are the same except that the visual has one additional row at the bottom of the table. Visual 5.5 is the same as Activity 5.4.)

2. A copy of Activities 5.1 and 5.2 for each group of three students

3. A copy of Activities 5.3, 5.4 and 5.5 for each student

4. Four signs labeled "Strongly Agree," "Agree," "Disagree," "Strongly Disagree"

5. Tape

6. Transparency pens

PROCEDURE

1. Tell the students that they will participate in activities to help them understand the relationship between economic freedom and a country's standard of living.

2. Tape signs labeled "Strongly Agree," "Agree," "Disagree" and "Strongly Disagree" a few feet apart from each other along a wall or on the board in front of the room. Tell the students that you are going to read several rules or laws a government might make. The students must decide how they feel about government's role in establishing each rule or law. When they have made a decision, they should go stand under the sign that best reflects their beliefs.

3. Read each of the statements below. Allow time for the students to move to the sign that best reflects their opinion. For each statement, record on Visual 5.1 the number of students under each sign.
   • Students may work in paid jobs only

from the hours of 3 p.m. to 11 p.m.
- No one under the age of 21 may buy cigarettes and alcohol.
- Everyone riding a bike or motorcycle must wear a helmet.
- The government will determine the jobs you will have as well as the school you will attend.
- All middle school and high school students must pay a tax on soft drinks sold in school vending machines.

4. Have the students return to their seats, and ask them to defend their positions. *Answers will vary but most will involve concerns over restrictions of their rights or freedoms.*

5. Display and read the definition of **economic freedom** on Visual 5.2. (Hide the other definitions for now.) Ask the students how the government rules and laws from the previous activity affect their economic freedom. *The rules and laws limit their economic freedom by determining when and where they could work or go to school, establishing taxes that reduce the amounts of money available for spending and saving, restricting what the students can buy and requiring them to buy certain items such as helmets.*

6. Explain that all economies have economic goals and that one of these goals is economic freedom. Different economies place different emphases on economic freedom. Market economies tend to place more emphasis on economic freedom, allowing consumers and producers to make their own decisions.

7. Write **standard of living** on the board. Discuss the following:
   A. What does standard of living mean? *The students will most likely talk about the number and kind of material things people have.*
   B. What does the standard of living look like for you? *Answers will vary and*

likely include such items as CDs, cars, TVs, clothes, video games, food, houses, DVDs, skateboards, computers.
   C. How might rules or laws restricting economic freedom affect a country's standard of living and the welfare of its citizens? *In general, laws that restrict economic freedom have a negative impact on standards of living and the welfare of citizens.*

8. Inform the students that they are going to test their hypothesis by doing a scavenger hunt for economic and geographic data. Before they can conduct their scavenger hunt, they must know what data to locate and what the data mean.

9. Display and read the definition for **gross domestic product (GDP)** on Visual 5.2. (Hide the definitions below GDP.) Draw the following table on the board.

	Country A	**Country B**
GDP	$1,000	$2,000
Population		

10. Ask the students which country in the table above has a higher standard of living and why. *The students will most likely say Country B because B has a larger dollar amount of GDP.*

11. Add additional information. For the population of Country A, write 50 and for Country B write 200. Display and read the definition of **gross domestic product per capita** on Visual 5.2, (hiding the definitions below it). Ask the students which country now has a higher per capita GDP and why. *Country A, because it has per capita – per person – GDP of $20. Country B has per capita GDP of $10.*

12. Tell the students that the standard of living is the amount of goods and services available per person in an economy. The standard of living is measured by per capita GDP. Ask which country has a higher standard of living. *Country A*

13. Discuss the following questions:

    A. What must happen to a country's GDP if the country wants to increase or improve its standard of living? *The country's GDP must grow faster than its population.*

    B. What kind of work force would a country need if it wanted to increase its GDP? What about the health of these workers? *The country would need a trained, educated and healthy work force to increase GDP.*

    C. What impact would new and improved capital goods – tools, equipment and machines – have on GDP? *The impact would be to increase GDP.*

14. Point out that gross domestic product and gross domestic product per capita measure material goods and services. These indicators do not measure factors such as health and education that affect the welfare of a country's citizens.

15. Display all of Visual 5.2 and point out that one way to measure a country's health is by looking at **infant mortality**: the number of babies that die out of every 1,000 born alive. The extent of education in a country is measured by determining its **literacy rate**: the percentage of people over age 15 who can read and write.

16. Explain that geographers are concerned with a country's level of **development**. Development is the process of improving people's material conditions through diffusion of knowledge and technology.

17. Tell the students geographers place countries in groups as **more-developed** or **less-developed**. Display Visual 5.3. Point out that all countries are at some point on this continuum. Tell the students that a literate, educated labor force is absolutely necessary for a country to move from a less-developed to a more-developed status.

18. Explain that when geographers and economists rank countries as more-developed or less-developed, they look at a variety of factors including infant mortality rate, literacy rate and the percentage of the population employed in **primary, secondary and tertiary industries**.

19. Tell the students primary industries collect and produce raw materials and agricultural products. Secondary industries manufacture products. Tertiary industries provide services. Ask the students for examples of each type of industry. *Answers will vary and include primary: raising cattle, fishing, growing grain, mining ore. Secondary: processing beef; making steel; producing automobiles, shoes or bread. Tertiary: restaurants, dry cleaning, car repair*

20. Point out that a larger percentage of the population in more-developed countries is employed in services and manufacturing. In developing countries, a larger portion of the population is employed in producing raw materials and agricultural products.

21. Divide the students into groups of three. Distribute a copy of Activities 5.1 and 5.2 to each group. Activity 5.1 has eight countries. You may substitute or add others, using data from The World Factbook of the CIA (at http://www.cia.gov/cia/publications/factbook/).

22. Display Visual 5.4 and review the list of indicators. Explain that **gross domestic product PPP** means that the gross domestic product data for several countries have been converted to a common currency, in this case, U.S. dollars. This allows a comparison of data across countries because all of the data are in dollars.

23. Instruct the students to complete Part 1 of Activity 5.2. Go over the answers.

    A. Which two countries have the highest GDP PPP? *United States, China*

    B. Which two countries have the highest GDP PPP per capita? *United States, France* Why do you think there is a difference? *China has more people.*

   C. Which two countries have the highest standard of living? *United States, France*

   D. Which two countries have the lowest standard of living? *Kenya, India*

   E. Which three countries have the highest percentage of people working in agriculture? *Kenya, India, China*

   F. Which three countries have the highest percentages of people working in industry and services? *United States, France, Russia*

   G. Which two countries have the highest percentage of the population below the poverty level? *Kenya, Mexico*

   H. Which three countries have the highest literacy rates? *Russia, France, United States*

24. Assign each group one of the eight countries. Tell the students to complete Part 2 of Activity 5.2. Go over the instructions and give them time to work.

25. When the students have completed Part 2, display Visual 5.4 again. Ask each group to share its answers. Ask the other groups to check the data on the visual and say whether they agree or disagree with the conclusion and explain why. *The groups will probably list India, Kenya, China, Mexico and Brazil as having lower standards of living with higher rates of infant mortality and a higher percentage of population employed in agriculture. These will be less-developed countries. The groups will probably say that the United States and France have higher standards of living with lower infant mortality rates and a higher percentage of population employed in service. These will be more-developed countries.*

26. Ask the groups how much economic freedom they think their countries have and why. *Answers will vary, but the groups will probably say that countries with higher standards of living will have*

more economic freedom.

27. Distribute a copy of Activity 5.3 to each student. Explain that the Index of Economic Freedom ranks the world's largest economies based on 10 categories including banking, monetary policy, property rights, government regulation, wages and prices, and government intervention in the economy. Point out that the lower the index score, the higher the degree of economic freedom in the country:
   1.00 to 1.99: Free
   2.00 to 2.99: Mostly free
   3.00 to 3.99: Mostly unfree
   4.00 to 5.00: Repressed

28. Display Visual 5.4 again. Write "Index of Economic Freedom" in the empty cell in the last row of column one under "Indicator." Ask the groups for the scores for their countries. Record their answers on the visual in the appropriate cells. *India 3.53, Kenya 3.26, Russia 3.46, United States 1.85, France 2.63, China 3.64, Mexico 2.90, Brazil 3.10*

29. Ask the students what generalization they can draw from these data about the level of economic freedom in a country and the welfare of its citizens. *Countries with more economic freedom tend to have higher rates of GDP and economic growth, and their citizens seem to have higher standards of living and better health.* Have the students compare this answer with their original hypothesis.

30. Distribute a copy of Activity 5.4 to each student and display Visual 5.5. Explain that this is a **choropleth map**: a map that displays data by political boundary. Areas that share a quality have the same color or shading. This choropleth map shows gross domestic product per capita. The darker the color in an area, the higher the per capita GDP. Remind the students that more-developed countries tend to have higher per capita GDP than

less-developed countries. Ask each group to locate their country to see if it is more-developed or less-developed.

31. Tell the students to use Activity 5.3 to write the Index of Economic Freedom score on or next to the appropriate country on the choropleth map.

32. Discuss the following:
    A. Where are most of the more-developed countries located? *Northern hemisphere* Less developed countries? *Southern hemisphere*
    B. What generalization can you make about a country's level of economic freedom and its level of development? *Less-developed countries tend to have less economic freedom than more-developed countries.*
    C. Its standard of living? *Less-developed countries tend to have lower standards of living.*
    D. Its quality of life? *More-developed countries tend to have healthier and better educated populations.*

33. Countries that place a high value on economic freedom are usually market-oriented. Why do you think so many countries in the world are moving toward more market-oriented economies? *Market economies tend to have high levels of economic freedom, which usually means a higher standard of living for the citizens as well as better health and a higher level of education.*

CLOSURE

34. Use the following questions to review the key points of the lesson:
    A. What is economic freedom? *The freedom for people to make economic decisions for themselves including how to spend or save their incomes, whether to change jobs or join unions, and whether to establish new businesses or close old ones*
    B. What is gross domestic product? *The total market value of all final*

goods and services produced in an economy in one year.*
    C. What is the standard of living? *A country's per capita GDP (gross domestic product divided by population)*
    D. What can be said generally about the level of economic freedom in a country and the general welfare of its citizens and why? *Countries with high degrees of economic freedom have higher rates of per capita GDP, and their citizens tend to have a higher standard of living. With economic freedom, people are free to make their own decisions about spending and saving, where to work, when to start and close businesses. With economic freedom, government regulation is usually limited.*
    E. What are the differences between less-developed and more-developed countries? *More-developed countries tend to be technologically advanced, are highly urbanized and wealthy, have a high percentage of their population employed in services and industry, have low rates of infant mortality, high literacy rates and more economic freedom. Less-developed countries generally have low rates of urbanization, tend to have a high percentage of the population employed in agriculture, have high rates of infant mortality, high rates of illiteracy and less economic freedom.*
    F. What are primary industries? *Industries that collect and produce raw materials and agricultural products.* Secondary industries? *Industries that manufacture or produce products* Tertiary industries? *Industries that provide services*
    G. Why are more countries moving toward a market-oriented economy? *Market economies tend to have high levels of economic freedom and a better quality of life for the citizens.*
    H. What is a choropleth map? *A map that displays data by political boundary. Areas that share a quality are given the same color or shading.*

ASSESSMENT

Distribute a copy of Activity 5.5. Instruct the students to read the directions and answer the questions.

1. What is Country X's standard of living? *$10,000 per capita*

2. Is Country X more developed or less developed? *Country X is more developed because its standard of living – per capita GDP – is $10,000 per person, and 86% of its labor force is employed in industry and services, with only 18% in agriculture. It has low infant mortality and a 96.2% literacy rate.*

3. Does Country X have more or less economic freedom? Support your answer with information from the table. *It is more free because its Economic Freedom Index score is 2.00. The lower the index number, the more free the country is.*

VISUAL 5.1
HOW DO YOU FEEL ABOUT GOVERNMENT RULES AND LAWS?

1. Students may work in paid jobs only from the hours of 3 p.m. to 11 p.m.

Strongly Agree	Agree	Disagree	Strongly Disagree

2. No one under the age of 21 may buy cigarettes and alcohol.

Strongly Agree	Agree	Disagree	Strongly Disagree

3. Everyone riding a bike or motorcycle must wear a helmet.

Strongly Agree	Agree	Disagree	Strongly Disagree

4. The government will determine jobs you will have as well as school you will attend.

Strongly Agree	Agree	Disagree	Strongly Disagree

5. All students must pay a tax on soft drinks sold in school vending machines.

Strongly Agree	Agree	Disagree	Strongly Disagree

VISUAL 5.2
DEFINITIONS

Economic Freedom refers to the freedom for consumers to decide how to spend or save their incomes, for workers to change jobs or join unions, for people to establish new businesses or close old ones, and similar opportunities for people to make economic decisions for themselves.

Gross Domestic Product (GDP) is the total market value of all final goods and services produced in an economy in a year.

Gross Domestic Product per Capita is a country's gross domestic product divided by the number of people who live there.

Infant Mortality Rate is the number of babies who die out of every 1,000 live births.

Literacy Rate is the percentage of people over the age of 15 who can read and write.

VISUAL 5.3
DEVELOPED AND DEVELOPING COUNTRIES

More-Developed Countries
- Usually technologically advanced
- Highly urbanized and wealthy
- High percentage of the population is employed in services and manufacturing
- Relatively low rates of infant mortality and high rates of literacy

Less-Developed Countries
- Changing from uneven growth to more-constant economic conditions
- Generally characterized by low rates of urbanization
- Relatively high rates of infant mortality and low literacy rates
- A high percentage of the population in agriculture

VISUAL 5.4
GEOGRAPHIC AND ECONOMIC INDICATORS

Indicator	India	Kenya	Russia	United States	France	China	Mexico	Brazil
Gross domestic product (PPP)*	$3.02 trillion	$33.1 billion	$1.29 trillion	$10.98 trillion	$1.65 trillion	$6.45 trillion	$942.2 billion	$1.38 trillion
Population	1.1 billion	32 million	143.8 million	293 million	60.4 million	1.3 billion	105 million	184.1 million
Per capita GDP (PPP)*	$2,900	$1,000	$8,900	$37,800	$27,500	$5,000	$9,000	$7,600
Population employed in agriculture	60%	75%	12.3%	2.4%	4.1%	50%	18%	23%
Population employed in industry	17%	N. A.	22.7%	24.1%	24.4%	22%	24%	24%
Population employed in service	23%	N. A.	65%	73.5%	71.5%	28%	58%	53%
Infant mortality	57.92	62.62	16.96	6.63	4.31	25.28	21.69	30.66
Literacy rate	59.5%	85.1%	99.6%	97%	99%	86%	92.2%	86.4%
Population below poverty level	25%	50%	25%	12%	6.5%	10%	40%	22%

Source: The World Factbook 2004, Central Intelligence Agency. Data are most recent available.
N.A. means not available

*GDP PPP is gross domestic product data for several countries converted to a common currency (U.S. dollars) based on exchange rates for the different national currencies that reflect purchasing power parity (PPP).

VISUAL 5.5
DEVELOPED AND DEVELOPING COUNTRIES

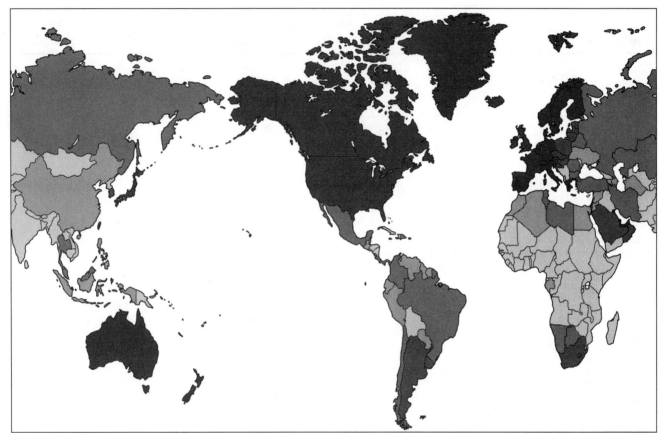

Base map by Mapquest

Per Capita GDP PPP	Index of Economic Freedom	Country
$55,100	1.71	Luxembourg
$37,800	1.85	United States
$29,700	1.98	Canada
$28,000	2.53	Japan
$27,700	1.79	United Kingdom
$27,600	2.03	Germany
$27,500	2.63	France
$26,800	2.26	Italy
$21,600	1.70	New Zealand
$19,700	2.36	Israel

Per Capita GDP PPP	Index of Economic Freedom	Country
$13,900	2.60	Hungary
$12,600	2.55	Uruguay

Per Capita GDP PPP	Index of Economic Freedom	Country
$5,000	3.64	China
$4,600	3.39	Paraguay
$3,900	3.28	Egypt

Per Capita GDP PPP	Index of Economic Freedom	Country
$9,000	2.90	Mexico
$8,900	3.46	Russia
$7,600	3.10	Brazil
$7,600	3.08	Bulgaria
$6,400	4.55	Libya
$6,000	4.09	Belarus

Per Capita GDP PPP	Index of Economic Freedom	Country
$2,900	3.53	India
$2,800	4.08	Cuba
$2,400	2.59	Bolivia
$1,900	4.54	Zimbabwe
$1,000	3.26	Kenya
$1,000	5.00	North Korea
$500	3.73	Sierra Leone

ACTIVITY 5.1
GEOGRAPHIC AND ECONOMIC INDICATORS

Indicator	India	Kenya	Russia	United States	France	China	Mexico	Brazil
Gross domestic product (PPP)*	$3.02 trillion	$33.1 billion	$1.29 trillion	$10.98 trillion	$1.65 trillion	$6.45 trillion	$942.2 billion	$1.38 trillion
Population	1.1 billion	32 million	143.8 million	293 million	60.4 million	1.3 billion	105 million	184.1 million
Per capita GDP (PPP)*	$2,900	$1,000	$8,900	$37,800	$27,500	$5,000	$9,000	$7,600
Population employed in agriculture	60%	75%	12.3%	2.4%	4.1%	50%	18%	23%
Population employed in industry	17%	N. A.	22.7%	24.1%	24.4%	22%	24%	24%
Population employed in service	23%	N. A.	65%	73.5%	71.5%	28%	58%	53%
Infant mortality	57.92	62.62	16.96	6.63	4.31	25.28	21.69	30.66
Literacy rate	59.5%	85.1%	99.6%	97%	99%	86%	92.2%	86.4%
Population below poverty level	25%	50%	25%	12%	6.5%	10%	40%	22%

Source: The World Factbook 2004, Central Intelligence Agency. Data are most recent available.
N.A. means not available

*GDP PPP is gross domestic product data for several countries converted to a common currency (U.S. dollars) based on exchange rates for the different national currencies that reflect purchasing power parity (PPP).

ACTIVITY 5.2
SCAVENGER HUNT

PART 1

A. Which two countries have the highest GDP PPP?

_____   _____

B. Which two have the highest GDP PPP per capita?

_____   _____

C. Which two countries have the highest standard of living?

_____   _____

D. Which two countries have the lowest standard of living?

_____   _____

E. Which three countries have the highest percentage of people working in agriculture?

_____   _____   _____

F. Which three countries have the highest percentage of people working in industry and services?

_____   _____   _____

G. Which two countries have the highest percentage of their populations below the poverty level?

_____   _____

H. Which three countries have the highest literacy rates?

_____   _____   _____

ACTIVITY 5.2 (continued)
SCAVENGER HUNT

PART 2

Assigned country _____

Write one or two sentences for the country you were assigned about each of the following, then decide if the country is more-developed or less-developed and explain the basis for your decision.
- Standard of living
- Welfare of citizens
- Level of development

ACTIVITY 5.3
INDEX OF ECONOMIC FREEDOM

Free	1.00 to 1.99
Mostly Free	2.00 to 2.99
Mostly Unfree	3.00 to 3.99
Repressed	4.00 to 5.00

Ranked by Index Number		Sorted Alphabetically	
New Zealand	1.70	Belarus	4.09
Luxembourg	1.71	Bolivia	2.59
United Kingdom	1.79	Brazil	3.10
United States	1.85	Bulgaria	3.08
Canada	1.98	Canada	1.98
Germany	2.03	China	3.64
Italy	2.26	Cuba	4.08
Israel	2.36	Egypt	3.28
Japan	2.53	France	2.63
Uruguay	2.55	Germany	2.03
Bolivia	2.59	Hungary	2.60
Hungary	2.60	India	3.53
France	2.63	Israel	2.36
Mexico	2.90	Italy	2.26
Bulgaria	3.08	Japan	2.53
Brazil	3.10	Kenya	3.26
Kenya	3.26	Libya	4.55
Egypt	3.28	Luxembourg	1.71
Paraguay	3.39	Mexico	2.90
Russia	3.46	New Zealand	1.70
India	3.53	North Korea	5.00
China	3.64	Paraguay	3.39
Sierra Leone	3.73	Russia	3.46
Cuba	4.08	Sierra Leone	3.73
Belarus	4.09	United Kingdom	1.79
Zimbabwe	4.54	United States	1.85
Libya	4.55	Uruguay	2.55
North Korea	5.00	Zimbabwe	4.54

Source: 2004 Index of Economic Freedom, The Heritage Foundation and The Wall Street Journal

ACTIVITY 5.4
DEVELOPED AND DEVELOPING COUNTRIES

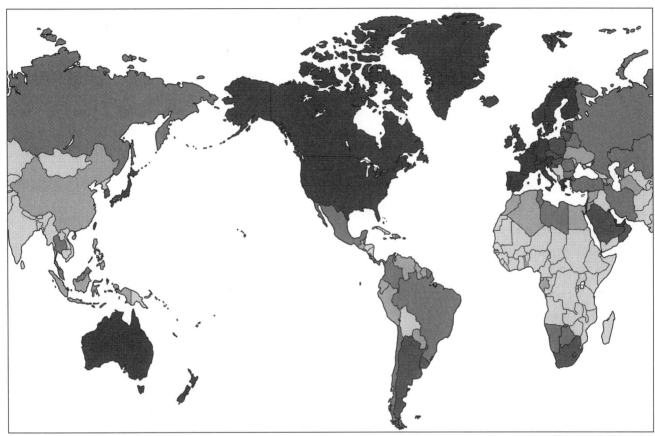

Base map by Mapquest

Per Capita GDP PPP	Index of Economic Freedom	Country
$55,100	1.71	Luxembourg
$37,800	1.85	United States
$29,700	1.98	Canada
$28,000	2.53	Japan
$27,700	1.79	United Kingdom
$27,600	2.03	Germany
$27,500	2.63	France
$26,800	2.26	Italy
$21,600	1.70	New Zealand
$19,700	2.36	Israel

Per Capita GDP PPP	Index of Economic Freedom	Country
$9,000	2.90	Mexico
$8,900	3.46	Russia
$7,600	3.10	Brazil
$7,600	3.08	Bulgaria
$6,400	4.55	Libya
$6,000	4.09	Belarus

Per Capita GDP PPP	Index of Economic Freedom	Country
$13,900	2.60	Hungary
$12,600	2.55	Uruguay

Per Capita GDP PPP	Index of Economic Freedom	Country
$5,000	3.64	China
$4,600	3.39	Paraguay
$3,900	3.28	Egypt

Per Capita GDP PPP	Index of Economic Freedom	Country
$2,900	3.53	India
$2,800	4.08	Cuba
$2,400	2.59	Bolivia
$1,900	4.54	Zimbabwe
$1,000	3.26	Kenya
$1,000	5.00	North Korea
$500	3.73	Sierra Leone

ACTIVITY 5.5
ASSESSMENT

Indicator	Country X
Gross domestic product (PPP)	$151 billion
Gross domestic product per capita (PPP)	$10,000
Labor force in agriculture	14%
Labor force in industry	27%
Labor force in service	59%
Infant mortality	8.88
Literacy rate	96.2%
Population below the poverty line	21%
Economic Freedom Index	2.00

You have been asked to prepare a research report for the United Nations about the level of development and economic freedom in Country X. Using the data above, answer the following questions:

1. What is Country X's standard of living?

2. Is Country X more developed or less developed? Explain.

3. Does Country X have more or less economic freedom? Support your answer with information from the table.

Lesson 6 - Joining Together That Which Has Drifted Apart

OVERVIEW

In this lesson, the students learn about the physical forces that move people on different continents further apart and the economic forces that bring them together. They read about the formation and breakup of two great continents, Laurasia and Gondwana, over 150 million years ago. They learn that continents are still moving today. They take the role of workers on these two continents who are producing pizzas and rugs. The students discover through their own calculations that even though the workers of Laurasia (representing more-developed countries) are more productive than those of Gondwana (representing less-developed countries), the workers on both continents can benefit from trade.

Geography: The movement of continents based on tectonic plates is the process that led to the development of mountain ranges, rifts and fault lines along which earthquakes and volcanoes may occur.

Economics: The production of goods is limited by the amount of natural resources, human resources and capital goods (resources) a worker or country has. The concept of opportunity cost determines which goods people should produce themselves and which they should acquire through trade with others. People's choices as consumers increase as a result of trade.

CONCEPTS

Geography
- Tectonic plates
- Continental drift
- Comparative advantage

Economics
- Productivity
- Production possibilities
- Opportunity cost
- Absolute advantage
- Comparative advantage
- Specialization

CONTENT STANDARDS

Geography
7. The physical processes that shape the patterns of Earth's surface

11. The patterns and networks of economic interdependence on Earth's surface

Economics
1. Scarcity: Productive resources are limited. Therefore, people cannot have all the goods and services they want; as a result, they must choose some things and give up others.

5. Gains from Trade: Voluntary exchange occurs only when all participating parties expect to gain.

6. Specialization and Trade: When individuals, regions, and nations specialize in what they can produce at the lowest cost and then trade with others, both production and consumption increase.

OBJECTIVES

The students will:
1. Describe the movement of continents and explain that this movement can lead to the formation of geographic features.

---

2. Construct a production possibilities table.

3. Determine the opportunity cost of producing a good.

4. Determine when a person or country has an absolute and/or comparative advantage in producing a good.

5. Explain that trade increases people's choices.

TIME REQUIRED

60 minutes

MATERIALS

1. Visuals 6.1 and 6.2 (**NOTE**: Visual 6.1 is the same as Activity 6.1.)

2. One copy of Activities 6.1 and 6.6 for each of the students

3. One copy of Activities 6.2 and 6.4 for each student in half the class

4. One copy of Activities 6.3 and 6.5 for each student in the other half of the class

5. Scissors and a stapler, glue stick or glue for each student

6. Chalk or masking tape

PROCEDURE

1. Ask if the students would like to visit Europe or Africa. Explain they had better hurry: These continents are getting further away from the United States every day!

2. Tell them that this lesson is about the physical forces that move people on different continents apart and the economic forces that bring them together.

3. Distribute a copy of Activity 6.1 to each student, and display Visual 6.1. Explain that the maps shows the major **tectonic plates**. Tell the students these plates are

sections of the Earth's crust that move as distinct units over the Earth's mantle.

4. Read the text that goes with the maps, and make the following points when appropriate, drawing the students' attention to the visual indicating the location, movements and features formed:
   • The east coast of South America appears to fit like a puzzle piece into the west coast of Africa. This is where geographers hypothesize it was attached when Gondwana was still intact.
   • The Himalayan mountain range was created when the Indian plate broke away from Africa and crashed into the Eurasian plate.
   • The Great Rift Valley runs from Syria to Mozambique between the African plate and the Arabian plate.
   • The midocean ridge in the Atlantic Ocean is between the African plate and the North and South American plates.
   • There is earthquake and volcanic activity around the Pacific Rim or the border of the Pacific plate (where it rubs against other plates).
   • Current activity has Africa moving north toward Europe, Australia heading north toward Asia, and North and South America moving away from Europe and Africa.

5. Tell the students they are going to participate in an activity that involves people on two different continents. Divide the classroom in half by drawing a chalk line (or using masking tape) on the floor between desks. Half the students should be on one side of the line and half on the other.

6. Tell the students they are now on two different continents: Laurasia and Gondwana. Explain that Laurasia and Gondwana are on two great tectonic plates that have separated along the chalk line drawn on the floor. Have the students move their desks across the floor away from the line toward the sides of the room to simulate this movement.

7. Read the following story to the students: Imagine that Laurasia and Gondwana drifted apart and developed very differently. Laurasia drifted into colder climates, so the people of Laurasia had to develop energy sources to keep warm. Later they used this energy to fuel machines to help them produce the goods they wanted. Gondwana drifted into warmer climates, so its people didn't need energy sources for heat. They never really developed machines and tend to produce most goods by hand.

8. Distribute a copy of Activity 6.2 to each Laurasian and a copy of Activity 6.3 to each Gondwanan. Distribute scissors and a stapler, glue stick or glue to each student. Have the students follow the instructions on their activities to cut out and make their production cards.

9. Distribute a copy of Activity 6.4 to each Laurasian and a copy of Activity 6.5 to each Gondwanan.

10. Have the students complete Part 1 of their activity. When they have completed their work, discuss the following:
    • Laurasians, what is the total number of pizzas you could produce in six hours? If you produced this many pizzas, how many rugs could you produce? *24 pizzas and 0 rugs*
    • Gondwanans, what is the total number of rugs you could produce in six hours? If you produced this many rugs, how many pizzas could you produce? *6 rugs and 0 pizzas*
    • How does the number of rugs you can produce change as you produce more pizzas? *It decreases.*
    • How does the number of pizzas you can produce change as you produce more rugs? *It decreases.*
    • Why does this happen? *It takes time to produce each good. Because time is limited, spending more time producing one good means less time is available to produce the other good.*

• Laurasians, as you turn over your production cards to the rug side, one at a time, what are the combinations of pizzas and rugs you can produce? *24 pizzas-0 rugs, 20-2, 16-4, 12-6, 8-8, 4-10, 0-12*
• Gondwanans, as you turn over your production cards to the pizza side, one at a time, what are the combinations of rugs and pizzas you can produce? *6 rugs-0 pizzas, 5-0.5, 4-1, 3-1.5, 2-2, 1-2.5 and 0-3*

11. Tell the students that the table they made shows the various combinations of pizzas and rugs it is possible for them to produce in six hours. This is a **production possibilities table**.

12. Have the students complete Part 2 of Activity 6.4 (Laurasians) and Activity 6.5 (Gondwanans). When they have completed the work, discuss the following:
    • Which combinations of pizzas and rugs are possible for you to produce in the time allowed? *Combinations D, G and I are possible for both countries.* (**NOTE:** The combinations on the two worksheets are not the same, but the letters of the answers are the same.)
    • Which combinations of pizzas and rugs are impossible for you to produce in the time allowed? *Combinations E, F and H are impossible for both countries to produce in the time allowed.*
    • What would make it possible to produce the combinations of pizzas and rugs that are now impossible to produce? *If more time were allowed or the workers were more productive — that is, each worker were able to produce more pizzas and rugs each hour*

13. Explain that the **productivity** of workers is measured by how much of a good they can produce in a given amount of time. On Laurasia, each worker can produce either four pizzas or two rugs in an hour. On Gondwana, each worker can produce either one-half of a pizza or one rug in an hour. Discuss the following:
    • On which continent are workers

more productive pizza producers? *On Laurasia, where they are able to produce eight times more pizza an hour than workers in Gondwana*

• On which continent are workers more productive rug producers? *Again on Laurasia, where they are able to produce two times more rugs than workers in Gondwana*

14. Explain that when workers in one region are able to produce more of a good than workers in another region, the workers in the first region are said to have an **absolute advantage** in producing that good. Since Laurasian workers are more productive than Gondwanans, Laurasians spend fewer hours making each pizza or rug. This means Laurasians have an absolute advantage in producing both goods. Ask the students if they think it is worthwhile in this case for the people of Laurasia to trade with the people of Gondwana. They will probably say no, but tell them things aren't always as they appear.

15. Have the students complete Part 3 of Activities 6.4 and 6.5. When they have finished their work, ask them "What is the **opportunity cost** of doing something?" *The highest-valued alternative you give up to do it*

16. For Laurasians, what is the opportunity cost of producing
    J. four pizzas? *Two rugs*
    K. one pizza? *Half a rug*
    L. two rugs? *Four pizzas*
    M. one rug? *Two pizzas*

17. For Gondwanans, what is the opportunity cost of producing
    J. half a pizza? *One rug*
    K. one pizza? *Two rugs*
    L. one rug? *Half a pizza*

18. Display Visual 6.2 to show these opportunity costs. Discuss the following:
    • On which continent is the opportunity cost of producing pizzas lower? *Laurasia*

    • On which continent is the opportunity cost of producing rugs lower? *Gondwana*

19. Explain that when the opportunity cost of producing a good is lower in one region than in another, the people in the first region are said to have a **comparative advantage** in producing that good. Note that while Laurasians are eight times more productive in producing pizzas, they are only twice as productive in producing rugs when compared with the Gondwanans. Thus the Gondwanans have less of an absolute disadvantage in producing rugs when compared with the Laurasians. The Gondwanans have a lower opportunity cost for producing rugs, which gives them a comparative advantage in producing rugs. Because the opportunity cost of producing pizzas is lower in Laurasia than in Gondwana, Laurasians have a comparative advantage in producing pizzas.

20. Explain that when people have a comparative advantage in producing a good, they can end up with more total goods by producing that good and trading some of it for goods in which other people have a comparative advantage. Concentrating production on one, or a few, goods is called **specialization.** Discuss the following:
    • Who should specialize in producing pizzas? Why? *Laurasians, they have a lower opportunity cost*
    • Who should specialize in producing rugs? Why? *Gondwanans, they have a lower opportunity cost*

21. Ask the Laurasians to turn all their production cards to the pizza side and the Gondwanans to turn all their production cards to the rug side to simulate this specialization.

22. Refer the students to Visual 6.2, and ask if trading one rug for one pizza is desirable for Laurasians. *Yes*

23. Explain that if the Laurasians produce the

rug themselves, it costs them two pizzas because they give up producing two pizzas. If the Laurasians trade for the rug, they give up only one pizza.

24. Ask the students if trading one rug for one pizza would be desirable for the Gondwanans. Why? *Yes. If the Gondwanans produced the pizza themselves, it would cost them two rugs. If they trade for the pizza it costs them only one rug.*

25. Have the students complete Part 4 of Activities 6.4 and 6.5, and then discuss their answers to Questions N (Laurasians) and M (Gondwanans). *For Laurasians the amounts of rugs that are possible with trade are 0, 4, 8, 12, 16, 20 and 24. For Gondwanans the amounts of pizzas possible with trade are 0, 1, 2, 3, 4, 5 and 6.*

26. Now discuss their answers to Questions O (Laurasians) and N (Gondwanans).
• For Laurasians and Gondwanans, which combinations of pizzas and rugs is it now possible for you to have that were not possible before trading? *Combinations B and C are now possible for both countries.*
Note: The letters of the answers are the same, but the combinations specified are different.
• Which combination of pizzas and rugs would still be impossible to have? *Combination E for both countries*
• How has trade affected the number of combinations from which you can choose? *It has increased the number.*
• Suppose you wanted to have the amount of pizzas and rugs in Combination C, what trade would you need to make? *Laurasians would need to give up four pizzas in exchange for four rugs, while Gondwanans would need to trade four rugs to get four pizzas.*

27. Have each Laurasian take one production card and each Gondwanan take four pro-

duction cards and line up along the border between the two continents.

28. Have each Laurasian trade with one Gondwanan, and then have them all pose as they shake hands on the deal. Tell them trading has once again joined these two great continents for the benefit of both!

29. Note that the continents of the former Laurasian continent – North America, Europe, and Asia – have developed economies, or more goods available per person, based on a high volume of trade among themselves. Meanwhile the main continents of the former Gondwanan continent – South America and Africa –- have less-developed economies, or fewer goods per person, with only limited amounts of trade. However, as this lesson demonstrates, all economies could gain by increasing trade where a comparative advantage exists. (**NOTE**: See Lesson 5 for activities on more-developed and less-developed countries.)

CLOSURE

30. Use the following questions to review the key points of the lesson:
A. What causes continents to drift or move slowly? *The continents are on tectonic plates that move across the Earth's mantle.*
B. What geographic features can result from the movement of tectonic plates? *Mountains, rifts, fault lines along which earthquakes and volcanoes are likely to occur*
C. What movement is a result of trade? *The movement of goods among people, countries and continents*
D. Why do people want to trade? *Because trade gives them greater choices and more goods*
E. Which goods should people produce and trade for other goods? *They should produce and trade goods in which they have a comparative advantage.*
F. When does a person or country have a comparative advantage in producing

a good? *When the amount of another good or service the person or country must give up is less than the amount others must give up, or when the opportunity cost is lower*

ASSESSMENT

Distribute a copy of Activity 6.6 to each student. Review the instructions and allow time for the students to work. When they have completed the activity, review the answers.

1. Which country has an absolute advantage in producing cheese? *France*
   Which country has an absolute advantage in producing beef? *France*

2. What is the opportunity cost of producing one pound of beef in Brazil?
   One pound of cheese
   What is the opportunity cost of producing one pound of beef in France?
   Three pounds of cheese

3. Which country has a comparative advantage in producing beef? *Brazil*
   Which country has a comparative advantage in producing cheese? *France*

4. Which good should Brazilian workers specialize in producing? *Beef*
   Which good should French workers specialize in producing? *Cheese*

5. Assume each French worker works only four hours a day. Complete the first two rows of the production possibilities table below. *See the table below.*

6. Assuming workers in each country specialize in producing what they do best and assuming each worker can trade two pounds of cheese for one pound of beef, show in the production possibilities table how this changes the amount of beef the worker can have. *See the table below.*

7. Explain why both countries would actually be willing to trade two pounds of cheese for one pound of beef. *If France produces its own beef, it must give up three pounds of cheese for each pound of beef. If it trades, it can get one pound of beef for only two pounds of cheese. If Brazil produces its own cheese, it must give up one pound of beef for each pound of cheese. If it trades, it can get one pound of cheese for only one-half of a pound of beef.*

Table B. Production Possibilities

Hours Spent Producing Cheese	4	3	2	1	0
Pounds of Cheese	*24*	*18*	*12*	*6*	*0*
Pounds of Beef (without trade)	*0*	*2*	*4*	*6*	*8*
Pounds of Beef (with trade)	*0*	*3*	*6*	*9*	*12*

VISUAL 6.1
CONTINENTAL DRIFT

Geological data indicate that around 250 million years ago there was a single, massive supercontinent on Earth. It extended virtually from the South Pole to the North Pole. Most of the rest of the surface area of the planet was covered with water. This continent has been named Pangaea. Pangaea was formed when several large tectonic plates – fragmented pieces that make up the Earth's crust – collided with each other.

Map based on plate tectonic maps by C. R. Scotese, PALEOMAP Project (http://www.scotese.com)

VISUAL 6.1 (continued)
CONTINENTAL DRIFT

But these plates never stopped moving. Spurred on by the heat of the planet's mantle and gravity, Pangaea was eventually torn into two great continents: Laurasia to the north and Gondwana to the south.

During the past 150 million years, these great continents also were torn apart to form smaller continents. Laurasia fragmented into North America, Europe and Asia while Gondwana separated to become South America, Africa, Australia and Antarctica.

Map based on plate tectonic maps by C. R. Scotese, PALEOMAP Project (http://www.scotese.com)

VISUAL 6.1 (continued)
CONTINENTAL DRIFT

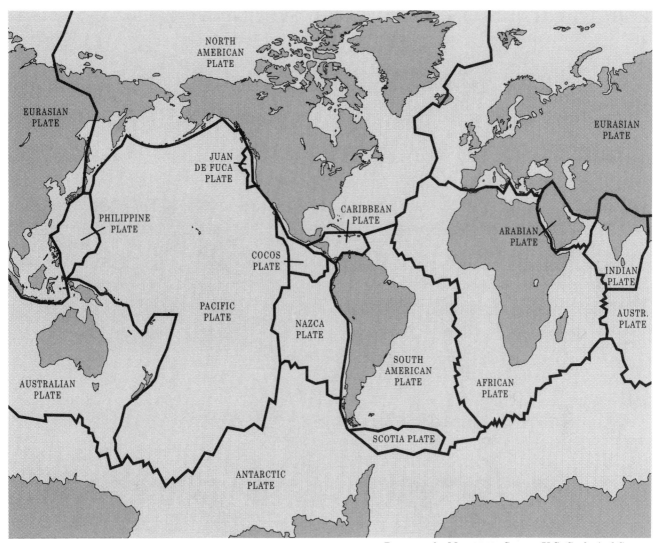

Base map by Mapquest   Source: U.S. Geological Survey

Today the plates on which these continents ride are still in motion. They are moving at approximately the same speed that your fingernails grow: about an inch each year! This may not seem very fast, but over millions of years the plates can travel large distances at this speed. Furthermore, geologists hypothesize that this movement has been responsible for the formation of great mountain ranges when the plates collide, great rifts on land and ridges in the oceans where the plates have torn apart and violent earthquakes and volcanoes where they come into contact and put pressure on each other.

VISUAL 6.2
OPPORTUNITY COSTS

FOR LAURASIANS

1 pizza

  costs

1/2 rug

OR

1 rug

  costs

2 pizzas

FOR GONDWANANS

1 pizza

  costs

2 rugs

OR

1 rug

  costs

1/2 pizza

ACTIVITY 6.1
CONTINENTAL DRIFT

Geological data indicate that around 250 million years ago there was a single, massive supercontinent on Earth. It extended virtually from the South Pole to the North Pole. Most of the rest of the surface area of the planet was covered with water. This continent has been named Pangaea. Pangaea was formed when several large tectonic plates – fragmented pieces that make up the Earth's crust – collided with each other.

Map based on plate tectonic maps by C. R. Scotese, PALEOMAP Project (http://www.scotese.com)

ACTIVITY 6.1 (continued)
CONTINENTAL DRIFT

But these plates never stopped moving. Spurred on by the heat of the planet's mantle and gravity, Pangaea was eventually torn into two great continents: Laurasia to the north and Gondwana to the south.

During the past 150 million years, these great continents also were torn apart to form smaller continents. Laurasia fragmented into North America, Europe and Asia while Gondwana separated to become South America, Africa, Australia and Antarctica.

Map based on plate tectonic maps by C. R. Scotese, PALEOMAP Project (http://www.scotese.com)

ACTIVITY 6.1 (continued)
CONTINENTAL DRIFT

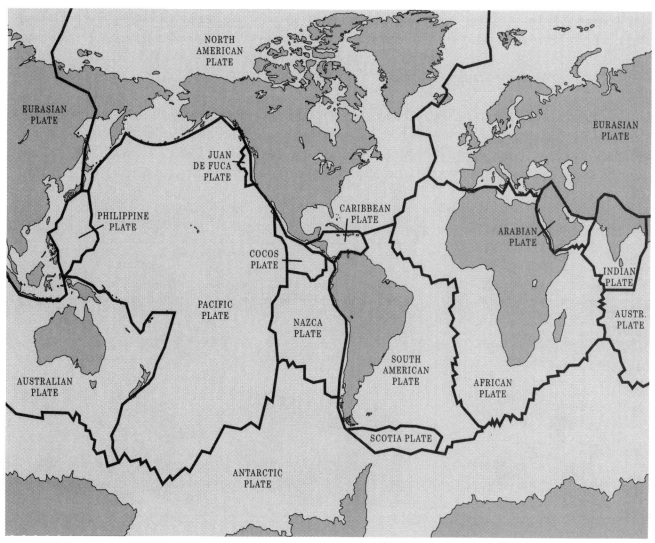

Base map by Mapquest   Source: U.S. Geological Survey

Today the plates on which these continents ride are still in motion. They are moving at approximately the same speed that your fingernails grow: about an inch each year! This may not seem very fast, but over millions of years the plates can travel large distances at this speed. Furthermore, geologists hypothesize that this movement has been responsible for the formation of great mountain ranges when the plates collide, great rifts on land and ridges in the oceans where the plates have torn apart and violent earthquakes and volcanoes where they come into contact and put pressure on each other.

ACTIVITY 6.2
LAURASIAN PRODUCTION CARDS

You live in Laurasia. Like most Laurasians, you like to eat pizzas and decorate with fine rugs. The more pizzas and rugs you can get, the happier you are. Unfortunately, making these goods takes time, and you have only six hours a day for production. In one hour you are able to make four pizzas OR two rugs, but not both.

Cut along the solid lines below. This will give you six production cards. Each card shows what you could produce in one hour. Fold each card in half along the dotted line with the pizzas and rugs facing out. Then staple or glue the two halves together. Lay the cards on your desk. Whichever side you have facing up shows what you are producing during that particular hour.

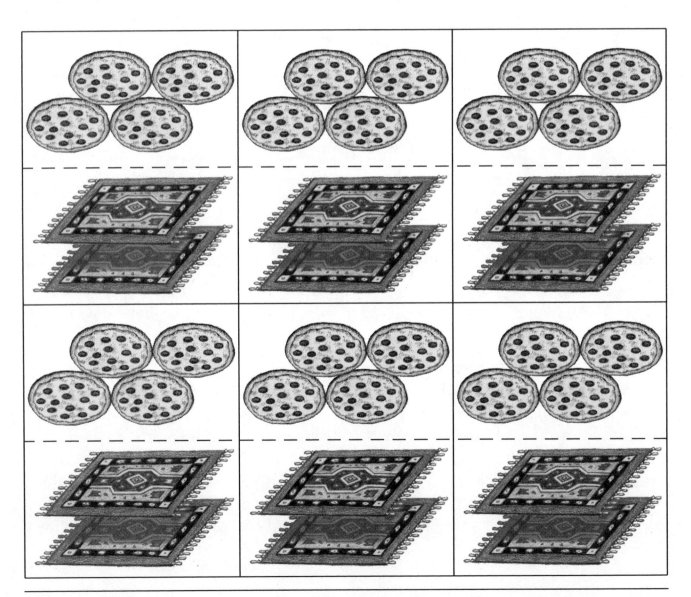

ACTIVITY 6.3
GONDWANAN PRODUCTION CARDS

You live in Gondwana. Like most Gondwanans, you like to eat pizzas and decorate with fine rugs. The more pizzas and rugs you can get, the happier you are. Unfortunately, making these goods takes time, and you have only six hours a day for production. In one hour you are able to make half a pizza OR one rug, but not both.

Cut along the solid lines below. This will give you six production cards. Each card shows what you could produce in one hour. Fold each card in half along the dotted line with the pizzas and rugs facing out. Then staple or glue the two halves together. Lay the cards on your desk. Whichever side you have facing up shows what you are producing during that particular hour.

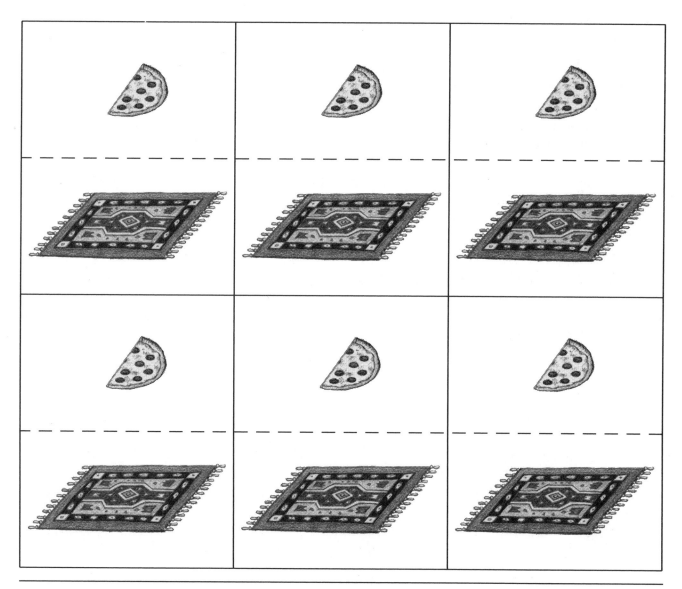

ACTIVITY 6.4
LAURASIANS WORKSHEET

PART 1. Production

A. Turn your production cards so that every hour is spent making pizzas. What is the total number of pizzas you could produce in six hours? _____ If you produced this many pizzas, how many rugs could you produce? ____ Write these two numbers in Column 6 of the table below. (Ignore the third row for now.)

B. Turn over ONE of your production cards. How many pizzas and rugs could you produce if you used your time this way? _____ pizzas and _____ rugs. Write these numbers in Column 5 of the table below.

C. Continue turning over the other production cards to the rug side, one at a time. Each time, record in the table below the number of pizzas and rugs you could produce.

Hours spent producing pizzas	6	5	4	3	2	1	0
Number of pizzas							
Number of rugs (without trade)							
Number of rugs (with trade)							

PART 2. Production Possibilities

Consider each of the combinations of pizzas and rugs below. Write "yes" next to the combinations that are possible for you to produce in six hours and "no" next to those that are not possible. Use your cards or the table above to help you decide.

D. _____ 12 pizzas and 6 rugs   **G.** _____ 8 pizzas and 6 rugs
E. _____ 0 pizzas and 16 rugs   **H.** _____ 16 pizzas and 10 rugs
F. _____ 20 pizzas and 4 rugs   **I.** _____ 4 pizzas and 10 rugs

PART 3. Opportunity Cost

The opportunity cost of a decision is the highest-valued alternative you give up. In other words, the opportunity cost of doing something is what you must give up to do it. Turn your production cards over one at a time and answer the following questions.

J. What is the opportunity cost of producing 4 pizzas? _____
K. What is the opportunity cost of producing 1 pizza? _____
L. What is the opportunity cost of producing 2 rugs? _____
M. What is the opportunity cost of producing 1 rug? _____

PART 4. Gains From Trade

N. Assume that you specialize in producing pizzas and can trade for rugs at the rate of one pizza for one rug. In the third row of the table in Part 1, write the number of rugs it would now be possible for you to have with each amount of pizzas listed.

O. Return to Part 2 and identify which combinations of pizzas and rugs it is now possible for you to have that were not possible before trading. _____

ACTIVITY 6.5
GONDWANANS WORKSHEET

PART 1. Production

A. Turn your production cards so that every hour is spent making rugs. What is the total number of rugs you could produce in six hours? _____ If you produced this many rugs, how many pizzas could you produce? ____ Write these two numbers in Column 6 of the table below. (Ignore the third row for now.)

B. Turn over ONE of your production cards. How many rugs and pizzas could you produce if you used your time this way? _____ rugs and _____ pizzas. Write these numbers in Column 5 of the table below.

C. Continue turning over the other production cards to the pizza side, one at a time. Each time, record in the table the number of rugs and pizzas you could produce.

Hours spent producing rugs	6	5	4	3	2	1	0
Number of rugs							
Number of pizzas (without trade)							
Number of pizzas (with trade)							

PART 2. Production Possibilities

Consider each of the combinations of rugs and pizzas below. Write "yes" next to the combinations that are possible for you to produce in six hours and "no" next to those that are not possible. Use your cards or the table above to help you decide.

D. _____ 4 rugs and 1 pizza   **G.** _____ 1 rug and 2 pizzas
E. _____ 0 rugs and 5 pizzas   **H.** _____ 4 rugs and 3 pizzas
F. _____ 2 rugs and 4 pizzas   **I.** _____ 2 rugs and 2 pizzas

PART 3. Opportunity Cost

The opportunity cost of a decision is the highest-valued alternative you give up. In other words, the opportunity cost of doing something is what you must give up to do it. Turn your production cards over one at a time and answer the following questions.

J. What is the opportunity cost of producing half a pizza? _____
K. What is the opportunity cost of producing one pizza? _____
L. What is the opportunity cost of producing one rug? _____

PART 4. Gains From Trade

M. Assume that you specialize in producing rugs and can trade for pizzas at the rate of one rug for one pizza. In the third row of the table in Part 1, write the number of pizzas it would now be possible for you to have with each amount of rugs listed.

N. Return to Part 2 and identify which combinations of rugs and pizzas it is now possible for you to have that were not possible before trading. _____

ACTIVITY 6.6
ASSESSMENT: Which Workers Are More Productive?

Table A. Beef And Cheese Production

	Beef	**Cheese**
Brazil	1	1
France	2	6

The table above shows the number of pounds of beef or cheese a worker in each country can produce in one hour. Given this information, answer Questions 1-4.

1. Which country has an absolute advantage in producing cheese? _____
Which country has an absolute advantage in producing beef? _____

2. What is the opportunity cost of producing one pound of beef in Brazil?
_____
What is the opportunity cost of producing one pound of beef in France?

_____

3. Which country has a comparative advantage in producing beef? _____
Which country has a comparative advantage in producing cheese? _____

4. Which good should Brazilian workers specialize in producing? _____
Which good should French workers specialize in producing? _____

5. Assume each French worker works only four hours a day. Complete the first two rows of the production possibilities table below.

Table B. Production Possibilities

Hours spent producing cheese	4	3	2	1	0
Pounds of cheese					
Pounds of beef (without trade)					
Pounds of beef (with trade)					

6. Assuming workers in each country specialize in producing what they do best and assuming each worker can trade two pounds of cheese for one pound of beef, show in the production possibilities table how this changes the amount of beef the worker can have.

7. Explain why both countries would actually be willing to trade two pounds of cheese for one pound of beef.

Lesson 7 - What A Difference A Tool Makes!

OVERVIEW

In this lesson, the students use problem-solving skills to make decisions about using productive resources. The students observe a simple production activity that gradually requires the use of more and more tools. After a short discussion regarding the use of capital goods (resources) and their importance in making workers more productive, the students participate in a group activity. Each group will role play being placed in a different physical environment to see what capital goods they might best use or create to survive. Following the simulation, the students speculate about what they think were the most important capital goods for their physical location and why.

Geography: Geographers categorize areas of the world by comparing characteristics of the physical environments (natural resources). These characteristics include the climate and soil, vegetation and animal life. Natural resources are scarce; so to raise their standard of living, humans must use their creativity and skill to make changes in their environment. They can make these changes by using tools. The ways people change or control the environment using human resources and capital goods can affect the level of population and prosperity in regions around the world.

Economics: The students review the concepts of human resources, natural resources and capital goods with an emphasis on how capital goods (objects people make and use to produce goods and services) can improve human skills, allow people to produce in more efficient ways and overcome limitations in their physical environment. The lesson also introduces the economic concept of opportunity cost, which people face whenever they must choose among competing demands for scarce resources.

CONCEPTS

Geography
Place
Region
Physical environment: tropical rainforest, deciduous forests, deserts, arctic tundra, taiga or coniferous forest, and tropical savannas

Economics
Productive resources
Capital goods (resources)
Human resources
Opportunity cost

CONTENT STANDARDS

Geography
4. The physical and human characteristics of places

8. The characteristics and spatial distribution of ecosystems on Earth's surface

Economics
1. Scarcity: Productive resources are limited. Therefore, people cannot have all the goods and services they want; as a result, they must choose some things and give up others

OBJECTIVES

The students will:
1. Describe how capital resources help people produce goods and services and improve a physical environment.

2. Predict why some capital goods are more useful than others in different geographic locations.

3. Identify the opportunity cost of using resources to produce a good or service when the resources could be used to produce other goods and services.

4. Describe the major characteristics of the six kinds of physical environments.

5. Explain how humans adapt to a physical environment.

TIME REQUIRED

60 minutes

MATERIALS

1. Visuals 7.1 and 7.2
   (Optional) Make a Visual of Activity 7.1

2. One copy of Activities 7.1, 7.3 and 7.5 for each student

3. One copy of Activity 7.2, cut into cards

4. Small box or basket (Place the cards from Activity 7.2 into the box or basket.)

5. One copy of Activity 7.4 (six pages) for each group

6. The following items for a demonstration:
   9 pieces of 8.5 x 11 inch construction paper
   3 pairs of scissors
   3 pencils
   3 state or country patterns

7. One backpack or bag containing the following items: jump rope, umbrella, panty hose, bed sheet, candy bars, pocket mirror, rain poncho, paperback book, sewing kit (needle, thread, buttons), bottle of water, eyeglasses, pencil

PROCEDURE

1. Tell the students that they will participate in an activity that will require them to use their knowledge of geography and their problem-solving skills. Before the activity begins, they will watch a demonstration that introduces some important economic content that may help them with their problem solving.

2. Make a grid on the board with three rows and three columns. Label the columns Round 1, Round 2 and Round 3. Ask three volunteers to come to the front of the room to assist you in a demonstration. Label each row with the name of a volunteer.

ROUND 1

3. Give each of the volunteers one sheet of 8.5 inch x 11 inch construction paper and ask them to make a silhouette of the state or country in which they live. Don't let them use any other materials, and require that they remain standing while performing the task. The students will most likely tear the outline. Note on the grid how much time it took for them to complete their silhouettes.

4. After the students finish, discuss the following questions:
   A. How well does the students' work represent the silhouette of the state or country in which they live? *Probably not very well*
   B. Why is this the case? *The students were tearing the silhouette from paper, so they were not able to be very accurate.*
   C. What could have made the task more efficient? Record the students' suggestions on the board or on a transparency. *Answers will vary and include sitting down at a table and using tools such as patterns and scissors.*

ROUND 2

5. Give each of the student volunteers another sheet of paper, a pencil and a pattern. Repeat the task. Once again, note on the grid how long it took for the students to make the silhouettes. Ask the class how the silhouettes in this round are different. *Likely more accurate*

ROUND 3

6. Now give each student volunteer another tool: a pair of scissors. Ask them to repeat

the task of creating the state or country outline. This time they may use the pencil, pattern and scissors – and they may sit down at a table or desk. Again, note on the grid how long it took for the students to complete the task.

7. When the students have finished, discuss the following questions with the class:

   A. How did the situation in this round compare with the first two rounds? *The students should point out that the edges of the silhouettes are likely smoother. The silhouette is probably closer to the actual shape of the state or country.*

   B. In which round were the silhouettes most accurate? *The third round*

   C. Were the students able to complete the silhouettes faster in Round 1 or Round 2? Why? *Most likely in Round 2, because they had pencils and patterns*

   D. Were the students able to complete the silhouettes faster in Round 3 than in Round 2? Why? *Yes. They had pencils, patterns, and scissors; they were able to sit at a table or desk.*

8. Explain that tools such as pencils, patterns and scissors are examples of **capital goods (resources)**. Capital goods are things people produce and use in the production of other goods and services. Ask the students for other examples of capital goods. *Answers will vary and can include factories, machines, overhead projectors, pencils and scissors.*

9. Explain that producing the silhouettes also involved **human resources**. Human resources are the quantity and quality of human effort directed toward producing goods and services: in this case, the students who made silhouettes.

10. Ask the students what happened when they were able to use more tools. *Their production was higher quality and they could produce faster: It took them less time to make a more-accu-*

rate silhouette. Reinforce the point that capital goods allow human resources to be more productive and to produce higher-quality goods and services.

11. Point out that **productive resources** are the natural resources, human resources and capital goods available to make goods and services.

12. Tell the students they will role play being lost overnight in an unfamiliar environment and making decisions about how to use productive resources to be rescued. Divide the students into six groups.

13. Distribute a copy of Activity 7.1 to each of the students.

14. Read through the handout with the students. Open the backpack and display its contents. Discuss each item and point out that some of the items might be used as they are for shelter, food and to help the students find their way. Emphasize that some items contain pieces or parts that might be useful – for example, the glass lenses or metal frames from the eyeglasses. Make sure the students recognize that they do not have to use an item as it is but may take it apart and use the parts.

15. Display Visual 7.1. Explain that each group will be "lost" in one of the locations on the transparency. While the students are reading over the descriptions on the visual, ask one student from each group to pick a Lost Location Card to determine where they will be stranded. *The Lost Location cards from Activity 7.2 should have been cut out before class and put into an envelope or small basket so the students can't read them while they're choosing the card for their group.*

16. Distribute a copy of Activity 7.3 to each student and review the instructions with the class.

17. Distribute a copy of Activity 7.4 (six pages) to each group. Ask the groups to use the information on their Lost Location card and the descriptions on Activity 7.4 to identify the physical environment/biome in which they are lost.

18. Each group should decide which items on the backpack-items list from Activity 7.1 could provide shelter, food and drink. They should also figure out how they would communicate with others who could rescue them from this physical environment.

19. Tell the students that they should use their handouts to take notes and make drawings of any new capital goods they develop to accomplish their goals. Give them 15 to 20 minutes to work. (**NOTE:** Some groups may have difficulty with this activity, depending on their physical environment. Visit each group and help them get started if necessary.)

20. When the time is up, ask each group to report the following:
    • The geographic name of its biome *Location 1 is a deciduous forest, Location 2 is a desert, Location 3 is a tundra, Location 4 is a tropical savanna, Location 5 is a tropical rainforest and Location 6 is a coniferous forest.*
    • How the group members planned to use their items for shelter, food and communication *Each group's answer will be different depending on the creativity of the group.*
    • Whether group members took things apart to make capital goods, which items they took apart and why *Answers will vary but might include eyeglasses to use the lenses for communication.*
    • Which item on the list was the most valuable for the group and why? *Answers will vary, but it is likely the most valuable item will have more than one use.*

21. Display Visual 7.2 and discuss some uses for the backpack items that the students may not have identified.

22. Explain that their decisions about how to use their items involved **opportunity cost**: the highest-valued alternative they gave up when they made a choice. When they used an item in one way to fulfill an economic want, they gave up using that item for another purpose. This second-best use is the opportunity cost. Ask the students for examples of a use they chose for an item and the opportunity cost of their choice. *Answers will vary; for example, if the group used the rain poncho for shelter, the opportunity cost might be using it for collecting drinking water.*

CLOSURE

23. Use the following questions to review the key points of the lesson:
    A. Which items seemed to be most useful to all groups? Tally the answers on the board. *The most likely answers will be the sheet or ponchos for shelter, the water and candy bars for nourishment, and the glasses and mirror for communication.*
    B. Was any item unused or useless for all groups? *Answers will vary.*
    C. Define opportunity cost. *The highest-valued alternative given up when a choice is made*
    D. Define capital goods. *Goods people make and use to produce other goods and services.*
    E. Describe the main characteristics of the environments in which the groups were located.
    TROPICAL RAINFOREST
    • *12 hours of direct sunlight a day*
    • *Trees more than 100 feet tall*
    • *A canopy of leaves that prevents all but 2% of the sunlight to filter to the ground*
    • *Vines traveling up tree trunks*
    • *More than 15 million species of plants and animals*
    • *High humidity*
    • *More than 150 inches of precipitation a year*
    • *Temperatures over 80 degrees Fahrenheit*

ARCTIC TUNDRA
  • *Located around the North Pole*
  • *Long winter*
  • *Fewer than 10 inches of rainfall each year*
  • *Permafrost*
  • *Plants with shallow roots and small leaves*
  • *Plants that require little sunlight*
  • *Animals with fat and fur*
  • *Animals that hibernate or migrate*

TAIGA OR CONIFEROUS FOREST
  • *Long, cold winters*
  • *Short, cool summers*
  • *Land with many lakes*
  • *Rocky soil*
  • *Many evergreen trees*
  • *Fewer than 25 inches of rainfall each year*

DECIDUOUS FOREST
  • *Physical environment in which most of the world's population lives*
  • *30 to 60 inches of precipitation each year*
  • *Four seasons*
  • *Good soil*
  • *Many deciduous trees*

TROPICAL SAVANNA
  • *Wet summer season six to eight months long*
  • *Dry, shorter winter season*
  • *Winter is still very hot with frequent fires*
  • *Grasses are the dominant plant*
  • *Acacia and baobab trees*

DESERT
  • *Low precipitation*
  • *Hot and dry*
  • *Great fluctuations in temperatures: hot in the day, cold in the evening*
  • *Most animals are smaller and able to dig a den or nest to escape the hot sun and conserve moisture*

F. How do humans adapt to their physical environment? *They use their creativity to develop tools to change the environment. They use resources to produce goods such as houses and clothing that help them adapt.*

ASSESSMENT

For homework or during the next class period, distribute a copy of Activity 7.5 to each student and go over the instructions. When the students have completed the activity, gather the most creative drawings or notes on new capital goods for surviving in the various environments. You could post them on the board according to their main purpose: shelter, food, drink or communication. *Answers will vary depending on the physical environment of the group.*

VISUAL 7.1
LOST LOCATIONS

LOCATION 1
A deep forest of trees filled with brightly colored leaves surrounds you. The ground is soft soil with numerous ferns and leafy bushes. There is a stream with round stones of various sizes. Squirrels and birds' nests are all around in the trees. The weather is slightly cool.

LOCATION 2
You are on rough, dry land with low thorny bushes. Cacti are in scattered rocky areas. There is a good supply of short, dry plants and shrubs. The pale soil is very dry. You notice a few birds and snakes, and you see some small holes in the rocks. It is very hot.

LOCATION 3
You are on a vast rolling land without trees. It is very cool, and the soil seems soft and mushy under your feet. Moss and lichen surround some scruffy berry bushes. A few pools of water appear in the distance where ducks are wading.

LOCATION 4
You are in the middle of many low hills covered with dry tall grass. There are several shallow ditches surrounding the area. There are a few trees sprinkled across the area, and the air is hot and dry. You can see a herd of elephants in the distance.

LOCATION 5
You are surrounded by dense vegetation with many layers of tall-canopied trees. Plants and vines are everywhere. You can hear lots of animals calling, and the air is hot and moist. You think you hear water rushing, but you can't see it through the leaves because it's so dark.

LOCATION 6
You are in a dense forest with spruce, pine and some birch trees. It is easy to walk around because the dense trees, dry soil and rocks – along with all the fallen pine needles that cover the ground – prohibit much undergrowth.

VISUAL 7.2
SUGGESTIONS FOR USES OF THE ITEMS IN BACKPACK

The **needle in the sewing kit** can be placed on a leaf and floated on still water for a compass. The needle will point north.

Paperback-book pages are good for starting a fire: Heat from the sun can be focused through the pocket mirror or eyeglasses. (You should read the pages before you burn the book!)

The **jump rope** could be used for tying up the poncho or other materials for shelter.

The **umbrella** is a shade from the hot sun of the desert or wind and rain in other biomes, but the wires might also be used for cooking utensils.

The **pocket mirror** could be used for signals or to attract attention.

The **panty hose** could be used to tie branches together for shelter or to tie fruit or other food up in a tree to keep it away from animals.

The **glass** from the eyeglasses could be used as a scraper or knife to prepare food or to cut leaves or small branches for shelter.

Of course, **water and candy bars** are important as your only source of food and water until you figure out what you can eat and drink in your biome.

The **water bottle** is the only container. Once the water is gone, you can still use the bottle to collect more water such as melted snow.

The **bed sheet** could be shelter from the sun in the desert or torn in strips for tying things together for shelter or used as a flag to attract attention.

ACTIVITY 7.1
BACKPACK ITEMS

You and the other members of your group have been on a sightseeing trip of various environments and have become separated from the rest of the class. You find yourself in a remote location in late afternoon. You realize you will not be able to walk to safety before it gets dark, so you make plans for spending the night. The leader of the field trip for your group brought a backpack. Here's the list of items in the backpack:

- Jump rope
- Umbrella
- Panty hose
- Bed sheet
- Candy bars
- Pocket mirror
- Rain poncho
- Paperback book
- Sewing kit (needle, thread, buttons)
- Bottle of water
- Eyeglasses
- Pencil

As a group, decide which of these items you can use for
- shelter for your group
- food and something to drink
- communicating with potential rescuers
- finding your own way home in the morning

Remember you may use the items in the backpack as they are, or you may change the goods to make them more useful or to make different tools. Assume you are wearing the same clothes that you have on or have with you in class right now.

ACTIVITY 7.2
LOST LOCATION CARDS

LOCATION 1
A deep forest of trees filled with brightly colored leaves surrounds you. The ground is soft soil with numerous ferns and leafy bushes. There is a stream with round stones of various sizes. Squirrels and birds' nests are all around in the trees. The weather is slightly cool.

LOCATION 2
You are on rough, dry land with low thorny bushes. Cacti are in scattered rocky areas. There is a good supply of short, dry plants and shrubs. The pale soil is very dry. You notice a few birds and snakes, and you see some small holes in the rocks. It is very hot.

LOCATION 3
You are on a vast rolling land without trees. It is very cool, and the soil seems soft and mushy under your feet. Moss and lichen surround some scruffy berry bushes. A few pools of water appear in the distance where ducks are wading.

LOCATION 4
You are in the middle of many low hills covered with dry tall grass. There are several shallow ditches surrounding the area. There are a few trees sprinkled across the area, and the air is hot and dry. You can see a herd of elephants in the distance.

LOCATION 5
You are surrounded by dense vegetation with many layers of tall-canopied trees. Plants and vines are everywhere. You can hear lots of animals calling, and the air is hot and moist. You think you hear water rushing, but you can't see it through the leaves because it's so dark.

LOCATION 6
You are in a dense forest with spruce, pine and some birch trees. It is easy to walk around because the dense trees, dry soil and rocks – along with all the fallen pine needles that cover the ground – prohibit much undergrowth.

ACTIVITY 7.3
SURVIVING OVERNIGHT IN THE WILDERNESS

Read the description on your group's Lost Location Card and look for clues to identify the type of physical environment or biome in which you are located. After you decide which biome you are in, use the information in Activity 7.4 to figure out what you must do to survive until you are rescued.

- What natural resources would you find around you?

- How cold will it become here at night?

- Is food readily available?

- Can you locate water that is safe to drink?

Taking the list of items in your group's backpack, see what capital goods you can make to help you build a shelter and survive.

You will share with the class your plan for surviving and the item from the backpack that you found most valuable.

ACTIVITY 7.4
INFORMATION ABOUT PHYSICAL ENVIRONMENTS

TROPICAL RAINFOREST

Rainforests are close to the Earth's equator and, consequently, get up to 12 hours of direct sunlight every day. However, the only plants that see the sunlight are the tallest trees (more than 100 feet). These create a canopy of leaves that allows less than 2 percent of the sun to filter down to the ground. Other plants have adapted to successfully compete for the light. One example of adaptation is that vines grow up the tree trunks toward the sun. Other plants such as fungus (mushrooms) have adapted to the shade. More than 15 million species of plants and animals have figured out how to adapt to this physical environment. More animals are found here than in any other physical environment. Monkeys, birds, snakes, rodents, frogs and lizards are everywhere; most of them stay up in the trees away from their predators. Rainforests are humid places with temperatures that rarely drop below 80 degrees and have more than 150 inches of precipitation each year. All this rain leaches nutrients out of the soil so the plants have to store the nutrients they need. When a plant dies or a leaf drops on the ground, the heat and humidity quickly decompose the debris and other plants quickly use the nutrients.

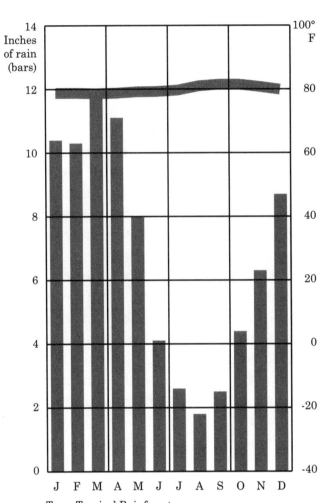

Type: Tropical Rainforest
Place: Manaus, Brazil
Source: WorldClimate.com

ACTIVITY 7.4 (continued)
INFORMATION ABOUT PHYSICAL ENVIRONMENTS

ARCTIC TUNDRA

Arctic Tundra is located around the North Pole. This physical environment has long winters and dark sunless days. The tundra gets fewer than 10 inches of rain a year. During the short summer, the snow melts but can't soak into the ground because of the permafrost. Permafrost is a layer of permanently frozen ground just below the few inches of topsoil called the active layer. Water from the melted snow pools on top of the land. The only plants that grow here – mosses, lichens, low-growing shrubs and some grasses – have adapted with shallow roots. Because the sun disappears for two months during the winter and provides only indirect light during the summer's 24-hour days, indigenous plants don't need much sun. Many grow under snow and their leaves are small, conserving moisture. Most of the animals adapt to the harsh climate with layers of fur and fat. They also adapt by hibernating or by migrating to warmer areas during the coldest periods of the year. The Arctic wolf, the brown bear and the musk ox are three animals that stay year round.

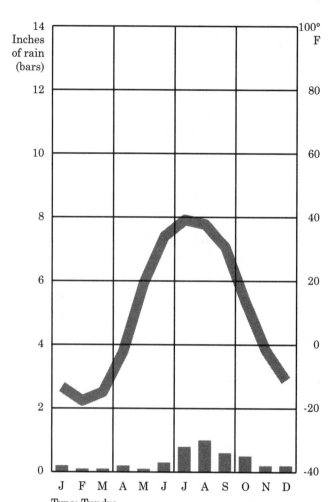

Type: Tundra
Place: Barrow, Alaska
Source: WorldClimate.com

ACTIVITY 7.4 (continued)
INFORMATION ABOUT PHYSICAL ENVIRONMENTS

TAIGA OR CONIFEROUS FOREST

Just south of the tundra is the physical environment called the taiga. Canada, Russia and Northern Europe are taiga regions. Winters are long and cold, and the summers are short and cool. Glaciers once covered this land. As the glaciers retreated, they left depressions for the many lakes found in taiga regions. The glaciers also left rocks and other debris, so the soil is rocky and gains few nutrients from the slow-to-decay pine needles that evergreen trees drop. These needles – the evergreen's leaves – also conserve moisture in an area with less than 25 inches of rain a year. Evergreens do well in taiga because they don't drop their leaves every year. This saves energy and nutrients for the trees in a climate that has poor soil and low sun. There is not much plant diversity here. There are four types of conifer trees: pine, spruce, fir and tamarack. In the southern part of taiga, you can find some deciduous trees such as birch and aspen. Animals include moose and bears, as well as bobcats, ermine, chipmunks and moles. One interesting aspect of this environment is that the lakes, ponds and bogs are perfect for breeding insects that, in turn, lure migratory birds that feed on the insects.

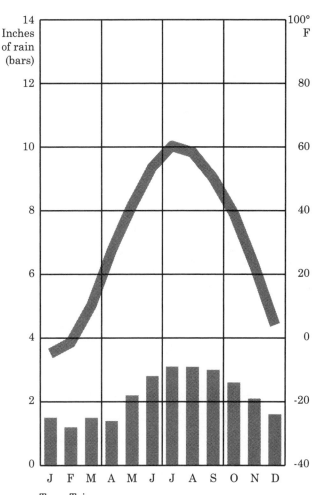

Type: Taiga
Place: Moosonee, Canada
Source: WorldClimate.com

ACTIVITY 7.4 (continued)
INFORMATION ABOUT PHYSICAL ENVIRONMENTS

DECIDUOUS FOREST

Between the cool taiga and the hot rainforest is the biome where most of the world's population lives. The midlatitude deciduous forest has four seasons, fairly steady precipitation year round – 30 to 60 inches a year – and good soil. Trees here such as maple, oak, hickory and beech drop their leaves every fall in preparation for winter. The leaves decompose and add nutrients to the soil. Consequently, most of the world's food is grown in this environment. Actually the plant life here is very diverse. It includes different kinds of deciduous and coniferous trees, smaller shrubs, wildflowers and grasses. Animals in this environment include large mammals such as bears, timber wolves, mountain lions, elk and bison. Over time, these animals have become harder to find because humans are destroying their habitats. Raccoons, squirrels, skunks and mice, however, have all adapted well to urban life.

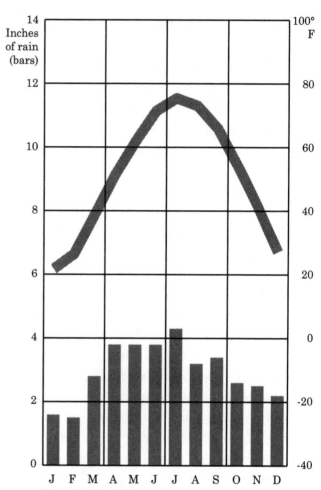

Type: Deciduous Forest
Place: Peoria, Ill.

Source: WorldClimate.com

ACTIVITY 7.4 (continued)
INFORMATION ABOUT PHYSICAL ENVIRONMENTS

TROPICAL SAVANNA

The tropical savanna is a biome marked by a wet summer season (six to eight months) followed by a short, dry winter season. Even though it is called winter, this season is still very hot and the frequent fires at this time keep the land clear of trees and replenish the soil. Grasses, therefore, are the dominant plant. Unlike treeless prairies, savannas have baobab and acacia trees. Savanna grasses survive the drought by storing water in their roots, as does the acacia tree. The baobab stores water in its trunk. Of course, animals of the savanna know this. The elephant uses its strength to tear open the tree for water when needed. Other animals in the savanna are wildebeest, warthogs, zebras, rhinos, gazelles, hyenas, cheetahs, lions, leopards, ostrich, mousebirds, starlings and weavers.

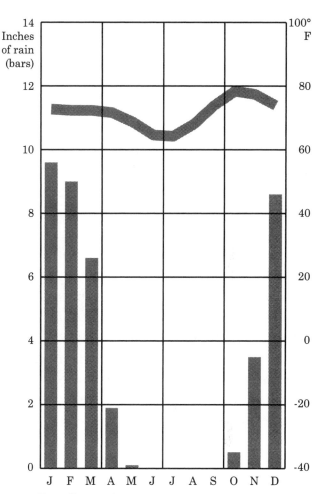

Type: Savannah
Place: Chipata, Zambia
Source: WorldClimate.com

ACTIVITY 7.4 (continued)
INFORMATION ABOUT PHYSICAL ENVIRONMENTS

DESERT

A desert is created when a geographic landform prevents an area from getting water. For example, the Himalayas prevent rain in the Gobi Desert in Mongolia because winds dump moisture from the air as they cross the mountains. A desert is similar to the tundra because of its low precipitation and wind. This physical environment is also similar to the savanna because of its winter drought. Because there is little moisture in the air, temperatures are high during the day but drop off steeply at night, making survival difficult. The desert has its own plants and animals. The plants are short grasses, sagebrush, creosote bushes and many different cacti. These plants have various ways of collecting and keeping water. Some have roots that go deep into the ground for groundwater. Others have roots that are shallow and run horizontally to collect water that lands on the surface of the desert. Still others like the cacti collect water in leaves. If people can get past the sharp needles of the cacti, they can have water. Most of the animals in the desert – such as reptiles, insects, birds and mice – are relatively small. However, there are also wolves and antelope. The largest desert animal is the kangaroo of Australia. Most of these animals can dig a den or nest to get away from the hot sun and conserve moisture.

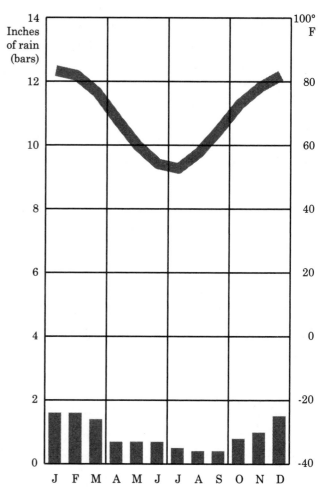

Type: Desert
Place: Alice Springs, Australia
Source: WorldClimate.com

ACTIVITY 7.5
ASSESSMENT

Write a diary entry about your group's adventure lost overnight in the wilderness. Use your copy of Activity 7.4 for characteristics and notes about the various locations and resources. The entry should include the following elements. You may add sketches or drawings, too.

• Describe at least three physical characteristics of the environment in which your group was stranded.

• Include a definition of capital goods and a description of a capital good your group used.

• List at least two capital goods – not necessarily from the backpack – that would be helpful to have if you lived in this environment permanently and explain why each good would improve your group's ability to survive.

• Choose another environment that you learned about and describe three items you would take along to help you survive in this environment. Explain how each item would be useful.

Lesson 8 - Ideas That Changed the World

OVERVIEW

In this lesson, the students learn about productivity and its connection to the standard of living. They learn about inventions that changed the world. The students make predictions about recent inventions and the impact of these inventions on productivity, standard of living and quality of life.

Geography: Geographers examine how groups of individuals and cultures adapt tools, machines and technology to overcome some of the challenges of their physical environment. People have long been inspired to solve problems of distance, climate and lack of resources that make living in some areas difficult. Geographers want to know how people's success with capital goods and technology can improve society and raise the standard of living in different areas and countries.

Economics: Economists look at the impact that capital goods, new technology and improved human capital have on the economy. Like geographers, they want to know how these factors affect productivity and ultimately, how they change people's occupational patterns, housing development, health and longevity, and overall standard of living.

(**NOTE:** Lesson 3 also covers the relationship of human capital and productivity to standards of living.)

CONCEPTS

Geography
  Standard of living
  Interaction with the physical environment

Economics
  Technological change
  Productivity
  Capital goods (resources)
  Human capital
  Standard of living

CONTENT STANDARDS

Geography
3. How to analyze the spatial organization of people, places and environments on Earth's surface

4. The physical and human characteristics of places

14. How human actions modify the physical environment

Economics
1. Scarcity: Productive resources are limited. Therefore, people cannot have all the goods and services they want; as a result, they must choose some things and give up others.

15. Growth: Investment in factories, machinery, new technology, and in the health, education, and training of people can raise future standards of living.

OBJECTIVES

The students will:
1. Define productivity, human capital, technological change, capital goods and the standard of living.

2. Explain the meaning of an increase in productivity.

3.   Explain the effect of increased productivity.

4.   Analyze the effect of technology and the use of capital on people's interaction with their environments.

TIME REQUIRED

60 minutes

MATERIALS

1.   Visuals 8.1, 8.2, 8.3 and 8.4 (**NOTE**: Visual 8.2 is the same as Activity 8.1.)

2.   One copy of Activities 8.1 and 8.3 for each of the students

3.   A copy of one reading and set of questions from Activity 8.2 for each group

4.   A large sheet of poster board for each group

5.   A set of markers for each group

6.   A sticky note for each student

PROCEDURE

1.   Explain that in this lesson the students will look at several inventions and consider their impact on productivity, the standard of living and the quality of life. To understand this impact, the students must understand the concept of **productivity**.

2.   Ask the students if they recall hearing the story of The Little Red Hen when they were younger. Remind the students that the hen wanted to bake bread. She tried to get her friends to help her, but they refused; so the hen did all of the work herself: She cut the wheat, she ground the wheat into flour, she mixed the ingredients and she baked the bread.

3.   Pose the following problem: If it took the hen eight hours to bake eight loaves of bread, how much bread would she be able to bake in one hour? *Some student may know the answer is one loaf. Continue by explaining that eight loaves of bread are to eight hours as X loaves of bread are to one hour or*
$8X = 8$
$X = 1$ *loaf of bread*

4.   Explain that one loaf of bread per hour is the hen's **productivity**. Productivity is the amount of a good or service a worker can produce during a given time period – in this case, one hour.

5.   Tell the students that the hen has purchased an electric dough mixer and learned new methods of production that allow her to bake 16 loaves of bread in eight hours. Ask the students how this changes the hen's productivity. *It increases the hen's productivity. Sixteen loaves of bread are to eight hours as X loaves of bread are to one hour or*
$8X = 16$
$X = 2$ *loaves of bread*

6.   Point out that the hen's **increased productivity** is a direct result of a new capital good (the mixer) and technology (the new production methods). Increased productivity – more output of a product per hour – typically leads to lower prices. What do lower prices for the hen's bread mean for people who want to buy bread? *People can afford to buy more bread, or people who couldn't afford bread before can probably afford it now.*

7.   Display Visual 8.1 and discuss the following with the students:
     A. What happened to the productivity of workers producing wheat and corn from 1800 to 1900 to 2000? *Productivity increased.*
     B. What happened to the productivity of workers producing cotton cloth from 1820 to 1859? *Productivity increased.*
     C. What happened to the hourly productivity of Ford auto workers from January 1913 to August 1913 to December

1913? *Productivity increased.*

   D. Why do you think these increases in productivity occurred? *Because people developed and purchased and/or invested in new tools – for example, the chain-driven assembly line – and/or invested in new production techniques. Point out that assembly lines such as Ford's allow people to specialize in one aspect of production. This division of labor increases productivity.*

   E. Predict what would happen to the prices of wheat, corn, cotton cloth and cars if workers were able to produce much more in the same amount of time. *Prices of these products would fall.*

8. Explain that if prices were falling, people could buy more of these goods, assuming the people's incomes remained the same or were rising.

9. Explain that economists and geographers are concerned with productivity because increasing productivity affects the **standard of living** in a country. Standard of living is the amount of goods and services available for each person in an economy. When productivity increases, more goods and services are available, and prices are usually lower. As a result, the standard of living improves. (**NOTE**: In real terms, national income for an economy is not the money payments in workers' paychecks but the number of goods and services people can buy with their paychecks. Real income depends on the economy's output. Output depends on productivity, so productivity is inevitably linked to the standard of living.)

10. Point out that the students identified two factors that affect productivity over time when they answered the questions about Visual 8.1.

   A. One factor is **technological change**. Technological change is an advance in technological knowledge that leads to new and improved goods and services and better ways of producing them;

for example, the discovery and application of herbicides and pesticides in agriculture. Henry Ford changed the technology of car production by having workers divide labor along a moving assembly line. Technological changes led to increases in productivity.

   B. A second factor that leads to increases in productivity is the use of new **capital goods (resources)**. Capital goods are things people produce and use to produce other goods and services. Sometimes these capital goods are the result of technological change: the rope-driven and chain-driven assembly lines in auto plants, tractors and steel plows on farms, and the cotton gin and power looms for processing and weaving cotton cloth.

11. Tell the students that a third factor affecting productivity is **human capital**: the quality of labor resources (people's knowledge, skills and experience), which can be improved through investments in education, training and health. A healthier, better-educated and trained population is more productive.

12. Explain that geographers study the ways people interact with the physical environment and how tools and technology allow people to overcome challenges the environment presents.

13. Distribute a copy of Activity 8.1 to each student and display Visual 8.2. Read the story to the class. Discuss these questions:

   A. What problem needed to be solved? *People were getting sick from drinking contaminated water. Disease could spread when many people used the same cup or drank from other shared sources of water.*

   B. Who came up with a solution? *Halsey Taylor*

   C. What was the solution? *The Double Bubbler water fountain and other fountain inventions*

   D. How did this solution affect productivity?

- Was it a change in technology?
- Was it a new capital good?
- Did it improve people's education or health?

The fountains were a change in technology and a new capital good. They improved people's health: Fewer people got sick from drinking contaminated water. Better health is an improvement in human capital, which leads to increases in productivity.

E. How did this solution allow people to overcome challenges presented by the physical environment? *It allowed them to get clean, and later cool, water in public places. Wall-mounted and recessed fountains were out of the way, which made it easier to move around in the building.*

F. How did this solution affect people's standard of living? *A healthier workforce is more productive. Increasing productivity improves people's standard of living.*

G. How did this solution affect people's quality of life? *Quality of life improved*

14. Explain to the students that these questions are similar to questions that the Finnish Technology Award Foundation asks in its search for "outstanding technological achievements that directly promote people's quality of life, are based on humane values and encourage sustainable economic development." Starting in 2004, the foundation honors an individual or research team every other year with the Millennium Technology Prize for an innovation based on scientific research in health care and life sciences, communications and information, new materials and processes, or energy and the environment. The prize was worth one million euros, or about $1.2 million U.S. dollars in 2004.

15. Tell the students that they will nominate candidates for the Millennium Technology Prize and then play the role of judges to select the winner. They will work in groups; each group will get information about an invention and its creator. They should read the information and answer the questions. Based on the reading and their answers, each group will make a poster to present their candidate for the prize to the rest of the class. Display Visual 8.3. Tell the students to be creative with their posters but to make sure they include answers to all the questions that apply to their candidate. Also tell the students to note that these questions are the same as the ones they answered to evaluate the impact of Halsey Taylor's Double Bubbler on people's productivity, standard of living and quality of life.

16. Divide the class into five groups, and give each group a reading from Activity 8.2, a large sheet of poster board and markers.

17. Allow time for the groups to complete their work.

18. Ask each of the groups to display their poster and to have a spokesperson present their candidate for the Millennium Technology Prize.

19. After the presentations, display Visual 8.4 and make sure each group covered the necessary information for their candidate. **(OPTIONAL)** You could wait to go over Visual 8.4 with the students until after they vote on the winner in Procedure 20.

20. Give each student a sticky note. Tell them to write their name on the note and place it on the poster for the invention they think should win the prize because it led to the greatest improvements in productivity, the standard of living and the quality of life. Remind the students that increased standard of living means more goods and services are available for each person in an economy.

CLOSURE

21. Use the following questions to review the key points of the lesson:

A. What is productivity? *The amount of a good or service a person can produce in a given time period.*

B. What is an increase in productivity? *The ability to produce more of a good or service in the same amount of time*

C. What factors lead to increases in productivity? *The increased use of capital goods, technological change, improved human capital*

D. What are capital goods? *Things people produce and use to produce other goods and services*

E. What is technological change? *An advance in technological knowledge leading to new and improved goods and services and better ways of producing them*

F. What is human capital and how can it be improved? *Human capital is the quality of labor resources – or people's knowledge, skills and experience – which can be improved through investments in education, training and health.*

G. Why is increasing productivity so important? *It leads to an increase in the standard of living.*

H. What is a standard of living? *The amount of goods and services available for each person in an economy*

I. How do technological change and the use of capital goods affect the way people interact with their physical environment? *Technological change and capital goods change the ways people use the limited resources in the environment and allow people to overcome the environmental challenges they face.*

ASSESSMENT

Distribute a copy of Activity 8.3 to each student and help them brainstorm the list of products. If they need help, suggest global positioning systems, satellite radio, TiVo, mapping the human genome and genetically modified food. Allow time for them to complete their work. *Answers will vary based on the products students choose.*

(OPTIONAL) Combine the articles to create a newspaper or magazine, or, if you have technology-savvy students, a computer or Internet presentation.

VISUAL 8.1
PRODUCTIVITY

Productivity is the amount of goods and services workers produce in a given period of time, such as an hour.

Table A. Number of Bushels Produced in One Hour

	1800	1900	2000
Wheat	0.26	0.92	25.00
Corn	0.29	0.68	33.34

Source: *Historical Statistics of the United States*, U. S. Census Bureau and U. S. Department of Agriculture

Table B. U. S. Textile Mills Output per Worker per Year

	1820	1859
Yards of cotton cloth	2,000	9,410

Source: "The New England Textile Industry, 1825-60: Trends and Fluctuations," by Lance E. Davis and H. Louis Stettler III. Included in *Output, Employment, and Productivity in the United States After 1800*, National Bureau of Economic Research, Studies in Income and Wealth, Vol. 30, 1966

Table C. Number of Ford Model T Chassis or Frames Assembled in One Hour

January 1913	August 1913	December 1913
No assembly line	Rope-driven assembly line	Continuous chain-driven assembly line
.08	.17	.67

Source: *American System to Mass Production, 1800-1932* by David Hounshell (Baltimore, Md.: Johns Hopkins University Press, 1985)

VISUAL 8.2
THE DOUBLE BUBBLER

In 1896, Halsey W. Taylor's father died from typhoid fever. Drinking contaminated water caused this disease. Because of this experience, Taylor spent his life trying to provide safe drinking water in public places. This led to the development in 1912 of the Puritan Sanitary Fountain and, in 1926, of the Double Bubbler. The Double Bubbler projects two separate streams of water that come together high enough for people to get a full drink of water without having to put their mouths on the projector. The Double Bubbler provided water in public buildings, schools and factories. The water was clean and safe for people to drink, which reduced the spread of disease.

Taylor also developed chilled-water drinking fountains. Initially these fountains used a 20-pound block of ice to cool the water. Later versions cooled the water by refrigeration. The early models were large and cumbersome. Eventually Taylor developed wall-mounted units and space-saving units that were recessed in the wall to allow for easier traffic flow.

A. What problem needed to be solved?

B. Who came up with a solution?

C. What was the solution?

D. How did this solution affect productivity?
- Was it a change in technology?
- Was it a new capital good?
- Did it improve people's education or health?

E. How did this solution allow people to overcome challenges presented by the physical environment?

F. How did this solution affect people's standard of living?

G. How did this solution affect people's quality of life?

VISUAL 8.3
CRITERIA FOR EVALUATING INVENTIONS

As your group creates its poster, answer the following questions. All questions may not apply to all of the inventions.

A. What problem needed to be solved?

B. Who came up with a solution?

C. What was the solution?

D. How did this solution affect productivity?
- Was it a change in technology?
- Was it a new capital good?
- Did it improve people's education or health?

E. How did this solution allow people to overcome challenges presented by the physical environment?

F. How did this solution affect people's standard of living?

G. How did this solution affect people's quality of life?

VISUAL 8.4
ANSWERS TO ACTIVITY 8.2

Barbed Wire

A. What problem needed to be solved? ***How to keep cattle out of farm land***

B. Who came up with a solution? ***Joseph Glidden***

C. What was the solution? ***Twisted or barbed wire for use in fences***

D. How did this solution affect productivity?
- Was it a change in technology?
- Was it a new capital good?
- Did it improve people's education or health?

It provided a way to contain herds of animals and to mark off areas of land. It was a change in technology and a new capital good. People could produce more beef and more crops in less time. Because people had access to more beef and more crops at lower prices, their health improved.

E. How did this solution allow people to overcome challenges presented by the physical environment? ***In the West, people didn't have access to material for wood or stone fences. This product allowed them to successfully contain herds of cattle and protect crops.***

F. How did this solution affect people's standard of living? ***There were more beef and more crops available. Food prices were lower. People could better enforce property rights.***

G. How did this solution affect people's quality of life? ***Ranchers spent less time herding cattle and keeping cattle out of cropland. Farmers no longer had to worry about having cattle destroy their crops. People, in general, were able to get food products at lower prices.***

VISUAL 8.4 (continued)
ANSWERS TO ACTIVITY 8.2

Penicillin

 A. What problem needed to be solved? ***Disease and death from bacteria***

 B. Who came up with a solution? ***Alexander Fleming and Howard Florey***

 C. What was the solution? ***Penicillin that could kill infectious bacteria***

 D. How did this solution affect productivity?
   • Was it a change in technology?
   • Was it a new capital good?
   • Did it improve people's education or health?
It improved people's health because people who were sick could be treated. This made the sick healthy again, and it also prevented people who were sick from spreading disease. Healthier people are able to be more productive. People missed less work time because of sickness. Penicillin was a technological change. It is not a capital good. It did not directly affect people's education.

 E. How did this solution allow people to overcome challenges presented by the physical environment? ***Bacteria in the environment spread disease. Penicillin helped limit the spread of disease.***

 F. How did this solution affect people's standard of living? ***Eventually, this product was available at a relatively low price. Sick people had access to this good.***

 G. How did this solution affect people's quality of life? ***People were cured of infections. There was less spread of disease. People lived longer in a healthier environment.***

VISUAL 8.4 (continued)
ANSWERS TO ACTIVITY 8.2

Telephone

A. What problem needed to be solved? ***How to transmit the human voice across telegraph wires***

B. Who came up with a solution? ***Alexander Graham Bell***

C. What was the solution? ***The telephone***

D. How did this solution affect productivity?
- Was it a change in technology?
- Was it a new capital good?
- Did it improve people's education or health?

Allowed individuals to speak directly across distances, meaning they could conduct business in less time. Led to the development of other communication products. The telephone was a technological change and a new capital good. It did not contribute directly to improvements in people's education or health.

E. How did this solution allow people to overcome challenges presented by the physical environment? ***People could communicate across long distances more easily.***

F. How did this solution affect people's standard of living? ***People were able to communicate much faster and easier. This reduced production costs for many businesses and made goods and services available at lower prices.***

G. How did this solution affect people's quality of life? ***People were less isolated. People in remote areas could communicate with others.***

VISUAL 8.4 (continued)
ANSWERS TO ACTIVITY 8.2

Self-Polishing Steel Plow

A. What problem needed to be solved? *Dirt sticking to the plow blade forcing the farmer to stop and clean the blade.*

B. Who came up with a solution? *John Deere*

C. What was the solution? *He replaced the cast-iron plow with a steel plow that cleared itself of mud and dirt as it plowed.*

D. How did this solution affect productivity?
- Was it a change in technology?
- Was it a new capital good?
- Did it improve people's education or health?

Farmers could plow the same amount of land in less time. Deere also mass-produced the plow, which meant more plows could be produced in the same amount of time. The new plow was both a technological change and a new capital good. It did not contribute to improvements in people's education. Because it increased food production, it did contribute to improvements in people's health.

E. How did this solution allow people to overcome challenges presented by the physical environment? *Farmers were having difficulty plowing the thick, sticky Midwestern soil. Deere's plow eliminated this problem with the physical environment.*

F. How did this solution affect people's standard of living? *Farmers' productivity increased which made more farm products available at lower prices.*

G. How did this solution affect people's quality of life? *People had more access to food, which improved their quality of life.*

VISUAL 8.4 (continued)
ANSWERS TO ACTIVITY 8.2

Dynamite

A. What problem needed to be solved? *People wanted to make it easier to blast rocks and drill holes to help in the construction of bridges, canals, buildings and other structures.*

B. Who came up with a solution? *Alfred Nobel, Ascanio Sobrero*

C. What was the solution? *Developing nitroglycerine into a commercially and technically useful explosive with a detonator that could be ignited by lighting a fuse*

D. How did this solution affect productivity?
 • Was it a change in technology?
 • Was it a new capital good?
 • Did it improve people's education or health?
Bridges, buildings, canals and other construction projects could be completed in less time and at lower costs. Dynamite was a technological change; and, if used in construction, dynamite is a capital good. It did not improve people's education or health.

E. How did this solution allow people to overcome challenges presented by the physical environment? *People were better able to perform such tasks as moving rocks, building bridges across bodies of water and constructing canals to move ships.*

F. How did this solution affect people's standard of living? *People, resources, and goods could be moved more quickly and at lower costs. Construction of buildings and so on occurred at lower costs. As a result, goods and services were available at lower prices and more goods and services were available.*

G. How did this solution affect people's quality of life? *Dynamite improved their quality of life because they had better quality transportation and better quality construction.*

ACTIVITY 8.1
THE DOUBLE BUBBLER

In 1896, Halsey W. Taylor's father died from typhoid fever. Drinking contaminated water caused his disease. Because of this experience, Taylor spent his life trying to provide safe drinking water in public places. This led to the development in 1912 of the Puritan Sanitary Fountain and, in 1926, of the Double Bubbler. The Double Bubbler projects two separate streams of water that come together high enough for people to get a full drink of water without having to put their mouths on the projector. The Double Bubbler provided water in public buildings, schools and factories. The water was clean and safe for people to drink, which reduced the spread of disease.

Taylor also developed chilled-water drinking fountains. Initially these fountains used a 20-pound block of ice to cool the water. Later versions cooled the water by refrigeration. The early models were large and cumbersome. Eventually Taylor developed wall-mounted units and space-saving units that were recessed in the wall to allow for easier traffic flow.

A. What problem needed to be solved?

B. Who came up with a solution?

C. What was the solution?

D. How did this solution affect productivity?
- Was it a change in technology?
- Was it a new capital good?
- Did it improve people's education or health?

E. How did this solution allow people to overcome challenges presented by the physical environment?

F. How did this solution affect people's standard of living?

G. How did this solution affect people's quality of life?

ACTIVITY 8.2
INVENTIONS THAT CHANGED THE WORLD

Barbed Wire

In the Eastern United States, farmers used stone and wood fences to separate cattle and other animals from farm fields. They did this to prevent the animals from eating the crops. In the 1870s, farmers were moving west across the Great Plains, but they didn't have access to stone and wood for fences. Although people in Texas tried to substitute ditches, mud walls and thorny hedges for fences, these failed to solve the problems that occurred between farmers and ranchers when cattle strayed onto croplands.

In 1874, Joseph F. Glidden of DeKalb, Ill., received a patent for fencing material made of barbs wrapped around a single strand of wire and held in place by twisting the strand around another strand. This was the most successful of hundreds of barbed wire designs that were eventually created. Glidden's barbed wire was strong and could restrain herds of cattle. Barbed wire changed the use and value of land in Texas and other western lands. People were able to fence in areas of land and claim property rights. This led to the enclosure of what had been known as the open range. Ranchers could still herd cattle, but farmers were able to protect cropland from the animals.

A. What problem needed to be solved?

B. Who came up with a solution?

C. What was the solution?

D. How did this solution affect productivity?
  - Was it a change in technology?
  - Was it a new capital good?
  - Did it improve people's education or health?

E. How did this solution allow people to overcome challenges presented by the physical environment?

F. How did this solution affect people's standard of living?

G. How did this solution affect people's quality of life?

ACTIVITY 8.2 (continued)
INVENTIONS THAT CHANGED THE WORLD

Penicillin

Bacteriologist Alexander Fleming discovered penicillin in London in 1928. He observed that a culture of staphylococcus bacteria had been contaminated by a blue-green mold. In areas where the mold touched the bacteria, the bacteria was dissolving. Fleming was very curious about the mold and grew some. He discovered that it killed many disease-causing bacteria. He named the mold penicillin and in 1929 published information about his study.

In 1939, Dr. Howard Florey and three people with whom he worked at Oxford University began intensive research and were able to show that penicillin could be used to kill infectious bacteria. In 1939, England was fighting World War II and didn't have the resources to produce the quantities of penicillin scientists needed to test it. Scientists in England contacted a lab in Peoria, Ill., in the United States. The lab was able to produce the necessary amount. In 1943, the tests were performed, and penicillin proved to be the most effective antibacterial agent of its time. Although penicillin was very expensive in 1940, by 1943 the price had fallen to around $20 a dose, and doctors used it to treat soldiers wounded on D-Day in World War II. By 1946 the price had fallen to 55 cents a dose.

A. What problem needed to be solved?

B. Who came up with a solution?

C. What was the solution?

D. How did this solution affect productivity?
- Was it a change in technology?
- Was it a new capital good?
- Did it improve people's education or health?

E. How did this solution allow people to overcome challenges presented by the physical environment?

F. How did this solution affect people's standard of living?

G. How did this solution affect people's quality of life?

Source: "The History of Penicillin," by Mary Bellis at http://inventors.about.com/library/inventors/blpenicillin.htm

ACTIVITY 8.2 (continued)
INVENTIONS THAT CHANGED THE WORLD

Telephone

On March 10, 1876, Alexander Graham Bell spoke these words into his experimental telephone: "Mr. Watson, come here. I want you." His assistant, Thomas Watson, heard Bell clearly. Bell had begun his work four years earlier while studying electricity. In addition to his interest in electricity, Bell was an expert in sound and speech. He combined his interests and began trying to develop a mechanism for transmitting the human voice. Although people were able to communicate by telegraph, they had to visit a telegraph office and could send only single messages, one at a time, over telegraph wires, which used intermittent current. Bell realized that transmitting the voice required continuous electrical waves of the same form as sound waves.

Bell obtained a patent for his invention on March 7, 1876. By the summer of 1877, the telephone had become a business. Bell's operation installed the first private lines, between businessmen's homes and their offices, and Bell Telephone Company – the predecessor to AT&T – was born. Bell understood the potential of the telephone. In 1878, he wrote, "I believe in the future wires will unite the head offices of telephone companies in different cities, and a man in one part of the country may communicate by word of mouth with another in a distant place." He was correct, but even greater things happened. Eventually families and individuals had access to phone service. Millions of people were connected by the telephone.

   A. What problem needed to be solved?

   B. Who came up with a solution?

   C. What was the solution?

   D. How did this solution affect productivity?
   - Was it a change in technology?
   - Was it a new capital good?
   - Did it improve people's education or health?

   E. How did this solution allow people to overcome challenges presented by the physical environment?

   F. How did this solution affect people's standard of living?

   G. How did this solution affect people's quality of life?

Source: AT&T at http://www.att.com/history/inventing.html

ACTIVITY 8.2 (continued)
INVENTIONS THAT CHANGED THE WORLD

Self-Polishing Steel Plow

John Deere began work as a blacksmith's apprentice in Vermont. In 1836, he immigrated to Grand Detour, Ill. Within two days of arriving, he had built a forge and was back in business. He learned from his customers that cast-iron plows they brought with them from the East didn't work well in the thicker Midwestern soil. They had to stop plowing often and scrape off the damp earth that stuck to the blade. Working with another Illinois immigrant from Vermont, Major Leonard Andrus, Deere invented a cutting blade that solved the problem. He shaped steel from an old sawmill blade and joined it to a specially curved wrought-iron moldboard (the plate that lifts and turns soil). He polished both parts of the new plow so that they were very smooth and damp soil wouldn't stick to them. This was Deere's Self-Polishing Plow, for which he received a patent.

His plow revolutionized farming in the United States. Farmers could plow more land in less time using Deere's plow. Deere continued to refine his designs because he knew if he didn't make improvements, someone else would. Deere also changed the way plows were produced. Instead of a blacksmith making plows when people ordered them, Deere mass-produced his plows and then went on tours selling them himself. By 1855, Deere was selling more than 13,000 plows a year.

A. What problem needed to be solved?

B. Who came up with a solution?

C. What was the solution?

D. How did this solution affect productivity?
- Was it a change in technology?
- Was it a new capital good?
- Did it improve people's education or health?

E. How did this solution allow people to overcome challenges presented by the physical environment?

F. How did this solution affect people's standard of living?

G. How did this solution affect people's quality of life?

Source: Lemelson-MIT Program at http://web.mit.edu/invent/iow/deere.html

ACTIVITY 8.2 (continued)
INVENTIONS THAT CHANGED THE WORLD

Dynamite

Alfred Nobel was born in Stockholm on Oct. 21, 1833. His father was an engineer who built bridges and buildings in Stockholm. In 1842, the family moved to St. Petersburg, Russia. Alfred's father wanted his sons to be engineers and join the family business. He sent Alfred to study in other countries. While in Paris, Nobel worked in the laboratory of Professor T. J. Pelouze, a famous chemist. An Italian chemist, Ascanio Sobrero, also worked in the lab. Sobrero had invented nitroglycerine, a highly explosive liquid considered too dangerous to be of any practical use. Nobel became very interested in nitroglycerine. He thought the substance could be used to blast rocks, drill holes and perform other construction work more easily, even though many safety problems had to be solved.

After visiting the United States, Nobel returned to Russia where he worked with his father to develop nitroglycerine as a commercially and technically useful explosive. Eventually, Nobel, his father and his brother, Emil, returned to Stockholm. Nobel continued his work and finally found that by adding silica (sand) to nitroglycerine, he could turn the liquid into a paste that could be shaped into rods the right size and shape to insert into drilling holes. He also invented a detonator (blasting cap) that a person could ignite by lighting a fuse. At the same time, the diamond drilling crown and pneumatic drill came into use. Together these inventions revolutionized the cost of blasting rock, drilling tunnels, building canals and doing many other forms of construction work.

   A. What problem needed to be solved?

   B. Who came up with a solution?

   C. What was the solution?

   D. How did this solution affect productivity?
   • Was it a change in technology?
   • Was it a new capital good?
   • Did it improve people's education or health?

   E. How did this solution allow people to overcome challenges presented by the physical environment?

   F. How did this solution affect people's standard of living?

   G. How did this solution affect people's quality of life?

Source: Nobelprize.org at http://www.nobelprize.org Copyright© 2004 The Nobel Foundation

ACTIVITY 8.3
ASSESSMENT

As a class, brainstorm a list of inventions such as the Segway, MP3 player, robots with artificial intelligence and picture cell phones. Write the list of products below.

Select one of the products from the list, and create a newspaper story and headline about it. Use resources in the library and on the Internet to write your article. Write the article in your own words; do not copy directly from your sources. Use a word-processing program to produce your story in a two-column format with the headline.

In the first paragraph of the article provide the following information:
- Who developed the invention?
- What does it do or how is it used?
- When was it developed?
- Where was it developed?
- Why was it developed?

In the second paragraph, answer the following questions:
- How does the invention increase productivity?
- How does it change the environment or allow people to overcome challenges in the environment?
- How does it affect people's standard of living?
- How does it improve the quality of life?

Lesson 9 - The Cost of Ignoring Economics and Geography

OVERVIEW

In this lesson, the students learn how geography affects the costs of achieving an environmental goal. They remodel the classroom using a map showing several companies located along a river. They participate in a simulation that shows the impact of putting waste into the river. They are given the task of determining the least-costly way to reduce this impact. The task is complicated by the fact that the costs of reducing waste aren't the same for all the companies, nor is the impact of their waste downstream. The students discover that when they take these factors into account, the cost of achieving an environmental goal can be greatly reduced.

Geography: The physical processes of dilution and decomposition work to reduce the impact of waste put into the environment. Relative location is also an important factor in the environmental impact of waste.

Economics: Economists study the costs of achieving an environmental goal and how these costs can be minimized. One strategy is a governmental policy based on economic incentives that achieve the goal at the lowest possible cost.

CONCEPTS

Geography
> Flow map
> Relative location
> Physical process
> Pollution

Economics
> Least-costly alternative
> Incentive

CONTENT STANDARDS

Geography
1. How to use maps and other geographic representations, tools and technologies to acquire, process and report information from a spatial perspective

7. The physical processes that shape the patterns of Earth's surface

8. The characteristics and spatial distribution of ecosystems on Earth's surface

14. How human actions modify the physical environment

Economics
4. Role of Incentives: People respond predictably to positive and negative incentives.

16. Role of Government: There is an economic role for government in a market economy whenever the benefits of a government policy outweigh its costs.

OBJECTIVES

The students will:

1. Construct a model of a region using a map.

2. Describe the physical processes of dilution and decomposition.

3. Explain why the location where waste is put into a river affects its impact downstream.

4. Explain that there are costs associated with cleaning up waste.

5. Determine the cost and impact of different governmental policies.

6. Describe how charges for putting waste into the environment create an incentive for people to reduce their waste.

TIME REQUIRED

90 minutes: 45 minutes each day

MATERIALS

1. Visuals 9.1 and 9.2

2. One copy of the appropriate page of Activity 9.1 for each group

3. One copy of Activities 9.2 and 9.3 for each of the students

4. Chalk or masking tape

5. 40 sheets of computer or notebook paper

PROCEDURE

DAY ONE

1. Ask the students if it is a good idea to breathe gases from the tailpipe of a car. *Most will say no.* Ask if they worry about breathing the air after a bus or car passes. *Some will say they do, but most will say the gases are less concentrated so the effect would be less intense.*

2. Explain that gases from a large number of cars can cause **pollution** and health problems in large cities such as Los Angeles. Pollution is the direct or indirect process resulting from human action by which any part of the environment is made potentially or actually unhealthy, unsafe or hazardous to the welfare of the organisms that live in it.

3. Ask the students if they can think of any natural forces that help reduce the bad effects of car emissions on the air we breathe. *Winds can diffuse the emissions over a large area, and rain can wash the emissions out of the air and carry them into the ground or water, where breathing them isn't a problem.*

4. Ask the students what other kinds of waste people put into the environment. *Garbage and sewage are likely responses, but also bring up other organic waste such as paper pulp and food-processing waste.*

5. Explain that waste is often put into our rivers, in part because water is another way to wash and diffuse waste. Much like the motion of the air by winds, the motion of water diffuses and dilutes waste so it is less concentrated. These physical processes of **degradation** or **decomposition** are the result of bacteria in the water that break waste down into less-harmful substances. So, as waste moves down a river, these processes reduce the impact of the waste on the surrounding environment. (**NOTE**: This lesson refers to "placing" or "putting" waste in a river instead of "dumping" the waste. Dumping has an obvious negative connotation – and gives the impression that using the environment as a site to dispose of wastes is somehow wrong or immoral. It is, in fact, physically unavoidable: Everything ends up back in the environment, either in the air, in the water or in the ground.)

6. Tell the students that this lesson is about

how best to control the amount of waste. Learning this requires not only some knowledge about the natural processes just described but also knowledge about the cost of reducing waste placed in the river in the first place.

7. Display Visual 9.1. Point out the following:
    • **Flow maps** are maps with arrows and lines showing how something moves or diffuses. This is a simple flow map of a river showing the direction the river is flowing and the direction waste will move. The map also shows the location of five companies – Acme, Bilt, Cogs, Dyno and Epay – and the city of Kleenville.
    • Acme and Bilt are at Location 1, Cogs and Dyno at Location 2, Epay at Location 3 and Kleenville at Location 4. The river is flowing from Location 1 to Location 4, as the flow arrows indicate.The locations are 10 miles away from each other. **Relative location** refers to the location of something relative to other things: This map shows the relative location of each company with respect to the other companies, the river and Kleenville.
    • Each company uses the river to dispose of its processing waste: waste it creates when it produces a product.

8. Set up the classroom based on this map.
    • The teacher's desk represents Location 4 in one corner of the room. The corner diagonally across the room represents Location 1.
    • Use a line of chalk or masking tape on the floor to represent the river.
    • Move desks so the river is wide enough for the students to easily move along it from Location 1 to Location 4.
    • Group three to four desks at each point along the river where a company is located – for example, at Location 1 on one side of the river to represent Acme and on the other side to represent Bilt.
    • Group five or six desks at Location 4 near the teacher's desk to represent Kleenville.

9. Assign roles for the students to play:
    • Three to four represent each company's board of directors (15 to 20 students total). Have them sit at the desks representing the location of their company.
    • Five students are river runners. River runners represent the physical processes of the river such as degradation or decomposition. One runner will stand in the river by each company location.
    • Five or six students represent citizens of Kleenville. Have them sit at the desks at Location 4.
    • The teacher will represent the head of the pollution-control agency for Kleenville and the surrounding area.

10. Distribute eight sheets of paper to each company. Tell the class that each sheet of paper represents one unit of waste.

11. Demonstrate the effect of the dilution and decomposition processes for the class by following the directions below. Tell the river runners to pay close attention because they will perform this function during the simulation.
    • Go to Location 1. Have an Acme representative hand the Acme river runner one sheet of paper. Tell the class this represents Acme putting one unit of waste into the river.
    • Walk slowly with the river runner "down" the river toward Location 2. Tell the river runner to fold the paper in half on the way down the river.
    • Stop at Location 2. Tell the river runner to show the class the paper. Explain that as the waste traveled down the river, it has been dispersed and diluted, as well as broken down by bacteria. The paper demonstrates that only half the original waste now affects the river.
    • Move on to Location 3 with the river runner. Once again, tell the river runner to fold the paper in half.
    • Stop at Location 3. Ask the river runner to show the paper and explain that only one-fourth of the original waste now affects the river.

• Ask the river runner to walk to Location 4 and fold the paper one last time. Now only one-eighth of the original waste still affects the river.

12. Explain that this demonstration assumes every time a unit of waste travels 10 miles in the river, or from one location to the next, roughly one-half is diluted or decomposed so the waste is no longer as harmful. Folding the paper represents this dilution and decomposition process.

13. Check the students' understanding of dilution and decomposition by having each of the other companies give their river runner one sheet of paper. These river runners should move down the river from their starting points to Location 4, folding their paper in half at each location.

14. When all the river runners reach Location 4, determine the total amount of waste at Kleenville by adding the amount for each runner plus the amount the Acme runner created during the demonstration in Procedure 11. *The total amount of waste is one and one-fourth units. This is determined by adding the original one-eighth unit of waste from Acme plus one-eighth unit from Bilt, one-fourth unit from Cogs, one-fourth unit from Dyno and one-half unit from Epay.* Unfold all the paper and return it to the companies. Discuss the following:

A. Based on the simulation, what generalization can the students make about the amount of waste a company puts into the river and its impact on the amount of pollution in the river at Kleenville? *Waste from companies that are located farther upstream, such as Acme and Bilt, have less impact on the amount of waste at Kleenville.*

B. Why is this so? *The waste has a longer distance to be diluted and decomposed.*

C. What does folding the paper represent? *The dilution and decomposition of waste*

15. Distribute a Company Cost Sheet (from Activity 9.1) to each company. Explain that each company's sheet shows how much waste it is currently putting into the river each day and the cost of reducing this waste. Because reducing or pretreating waste costs money, the companies prefer to put all their waste into the river.

16. Tell the class they are going to simulate what happens if there are no restrictions on the use of the river: Each company can put all its waste there.

17. Run the simulation.
• Have each company hand its river runner one sheet of paper for each unit of waste it is currently creating. *Each company is creating eight units of waste, so each runner should get eight sheets of paper.*
• Have the river runners move down the river and fold each sheet of "waste" in half as they reach a new location.
• Once they reach Kleenville, the river runners should pile all the waste (folded appropriately) on the teacher's desk.
• Have the citizens of Kleenville calculate and announce the total amount of waste affecting the river at Kleenville. *10 units: two from Acme and Bilt representing one-eighth of 16 units, four from Cogs and Dyno representing one-fourth of 16 units and four from Epay representing one-half of eight units.*

18. As the head of the pollution-control agency, announce that 10 units is just too much. Explain that any amount above five units makes the river smelly and could result in bad health effects for people who use river water to drink, cook, bathe and swim. To avoid these problems, the amount of waste reaching Kleenville must be reduced to five units. Discuss the following questions:
A. What must be done to achieve this goal? *Some or all of the companies must reduce the amount of waste they put in the river.*

B. What are some ways the companies could accomplish this? *Answers will vary and include installing pollution-control equipment that collects the waste for disposal elsewhere or transforms it with some treatment into less harmful substances, making the production process more efficient so it creates less waste, making changes in the inputs companies use or in the nature of the output itself that reduces waste – for example, making potato chips from unpeeled potatoes instead of peeling the potatoes first and then disposing of the skin.*

19. Explain that while companies could use any of these methods to reduce waste, all the measures have costs such as payments for control equipment. These costs are shown on each company's Cost Sheet. Tell the company representatives to look at their sheets. Point out that all companies do not have the same costs because some companies might be able to adjust their production processes more cheaply than others, perhaps because of the kind of products that they produce or because they have more modern machinery than some of the other plants.

20. Have each company read out loud the cost of reducing its waste by one unit and then the cost of reducing another unit. Point out that by making some rather simple adjustments, the companies can reduce the first few units of waste fairly cheaply, but as they try to reduce more, they typically must make more complex and expensive adjustments.

21. Have the class suggest a policy that would cut the amount of waste reaching Kleenville to five units, or half of what it is without any restrictions. Point out the following:
    • The most likely suggestion the students will make is to have every company reduce its waste by one-half. This will reduce the amount reaching Kleenville

to five units. If necessary, demonstrate by having the students go through the simulation again, with each river runner receiving four pieces of paper.
    • If the students suggest other options, conduct another round of the simulation to check whether the suggested option actually reduces to five units the amount of waste that reaches Kleenville.

22. Tell the students that each company must reduce its waste by one-half. Have each company calculate its cost of reducing waste by four units. Ask a representative from each company to share the answer, and have one of the Kleenville citizens add the amounts as they are announced.
    Acme: $10 ($1 + $2 + $3 + $4)
    Bilt: $5 ($1 + $1 + $1 + $2)
    Cogs: $10 ($1 + $2 + $3 + $4)
    Dyno: $10 ($1+$2+$3+$4)
    Epay: $5 ($1+$1+$1+$2)

23. Ask the Kleenville citizens to give the tally. Note that the total cost of reducing waste by one-half is $40.

24. Point out that having each company reduce waste by one-half reduces the total waste to 20 units. However, having Acme and Bilt eliminate waste completely and Cogs reduce its waste by one-half would also cut total waste placed in the river to 20 units. But the amount of waste actually reaching Kleenville would be seven units, not five. Discuss the following:
    A. Why, if 20 units of waste are going into the river in both examples, is the amount of pollution in the river at Kleenville different? *It is important which companies are doing the reducing because the impact of each is different downstream.*
    B. Why is the impact for each company different? *The further downstream the waste moves before reaching Kleenville, the more opportunity for decomposition and dilution, which reduces the amount of waste in the river at Kleenville.*

25. Conclude that a government regulation requiring all the companies to reduce their waste by one-half achieves the goal of reducing waste at Kleenville to five units. Ask the students, rhetorically, if there is a way to do this for less than $40.

26. Distribute a copy of Activity 9.2 to each student and display Visual 9.2. Review the directions. Have students complete Activity 9.2 for homework for Day Two.

DAY TWO

27. Have the students refer to their completed Activity 9.2.
    A. Ask how many found a combination that reduced the amount of waste reaching Kleenville to five units at a cost of less than $40. *Answers will vary.*
    B. Ask the students to present their solutions. *Answers will vary. Have the class check a few to make sure the students have calculated correctly the costs and the amount of waste reaching Kleenville.*
    C. To accomplish the goal of reducing waste reaching Kleenville to five units at a cost of less than $40, which companies had to reduce waste by more than four units? Why? *Bilt and Epay, because their costs for reducing waste are less than the costs for the other three companies*
    D. For which company does a reduction in waste placed in the river result in the greatest reduction of waste reaching Kleenville? Why? *Epay. This company is the closest to Kleenville, so there is less dilution and degradation of its wastes.*

28. Explain that a simple policy, such as having each company reduce its waste by one-half, ignores the economic fact that some companies may be able to reduce waste at lower costs than others. Such a policy also ignores the geographic reality of dilution and decomposition: A one-unit reduction of waste by companies closer to Kleenville has a bigger impact on pollution at Kleenville than the same reduction by companies farther away.

29. Tell the students that the **least-costly alternative** is the alternative that achieves a given objective at the lowest cost (also called the **cost-effective choice**). For the firms in this example and for the people of Kleenville, the least-costly alternative is the option that achieves the goal of five units of waste for the least possible cost. The least-costly alternative is for Acme to reduce waste by one unit, Bilt to reduce waste by three units, Cogs and Dyno each to reduce waste by two units and Epay to reduce waste by seven units.

30. Show that the total cost of this alternative is $26. *Acme $1, Bilt $3, Cogs $3, Dyno $3 and Epay $16*

31. Show that this alternative reduces the total waste at Kleenville to five units. *One and one-half units from the 12 units put in by Acme and Bilt, three units from the 12 units put in by Cogs and Dyno and one-half unit from the one unit put in by Epay*

32. Point out that ultimately Bilt and Epay reduce more with the least-costly alternative because they have lower costs. Cogs and Dyno reduce more than Acme even though they have the same costs because Acme is farther away from Kleenville. Epay does the most reduction because it not only has lower costs but is also the closest to Kleenville.

33. Congratulate the students who were able to come up with the least-costly alternative. Tell the class that this is a hard problem because of the different costs and locations. However, when these factors – the first economic and the second geographic – are taken into account, achieving an environmental goal (here, no more than five units of waste at Kleenville) can be obtained at a much lower cost ($26 versus $40). In the real world, these figures would be in millions of dollars, so ignoring economics and geography would be very costly.

34. Ask the students how hard it would have been to find the least-costly alternative if they did not know the costs of waste reduction for each company. *Most of the students would say it is impossible.*

35. Explain that this is the case in the real world. Companies keep such information to themselves and may argue that their costs are very high – even when they are not – so pollution-control agencies won't force them to reduce their waste. However, there is a way the pollution-control agency can still get the least-costly alternative.

36. Refer to Visual 9.2 and discuss the following questions:
   A. If the agency required Acme to pay a charge of $2.50 for each unit of waste it put in the river, how many units would Acme put in? Why? *Only six units. It would choose to clean up the first two units of waste because this would cost less – $1.00 and $2.00 respectively – than paying the charge. The remaining six units cost more to clean up than the charge, so it is cheaper for Acme just to put them in the river and pay the charge.*
   B. What if the charge were higher, for example $4.50? *Acme would choose to clean up the first four units because doing so costs less than $4.50 a unit.*

37. Explain that by raising the charge for putting waste in the river, the pollution-control agency creates an **incentive** for each company to clean up more of its waste. An incentive is a reward or penalty that can influence people's choices and behavior. Here the incentive is a charge for putting waste into the river. A company will continue to put waste in the river only if the penalty (the charge) is less than the cost of cleaning up a unit of waste.

38. Explain that the pollution-control agency knows – because of the dilution and decomposition processes – that waste from Epay has twice the impact at Kleenville as

waste from Cogs and Dyno and four times the impact of waste from Acme and Bilt. This suggests that the companies should be charged different amounts based on the impact of their waste. In this case, whatever amount the agency decides to charge Acme and Bilt, the amount for Cogs and Dyno should be twice as high, since their waste has twice the impact, and the charge for Epay should be four times as high. Discuss the following:
   A. Suppose the pollution-control agency sets a charge of $2.20 for each waste unit Acme and Bilt put into the river; twice this amount, or $4.40, for each unit from Cogs and Dyno; and four times this amount, or $8.80, for each unit from Epay. How would each company react to these charges? *Acme would clean up two units, Bilt would clean up four units, Cogs would clean up four units, Dyno would clean up four units and Epay would clean up all eight units.*
   B. How much waste would reach Kleenville? *Only three and one-fourth units: one and one-fourth units from the 10 put in by Acme and Bilt (10 x 1/8) and two units from the eight put in by Cogs and Dyno (8 x 1/4)*

39. Point out that this is more reduction than necessary, given the goal of five units at Kleenville. Ask the students how the charge should be adjusted to achieve the goal. *Since the firms are reducing more waste than is necessary, the agency should decrease the charge to lower the incentive to reduce so much.*

40. Ask the students to determine how much each company would reduce their waste if the charge were $1.20 for Acme and Bilt, $2.40 ($1.20 x 2) for Cogs and Dyno and $4.80 ($1.20 x 4) for Epay. *Acme, one unit; Bilt, three units; Cogs, two units; Dyno, two units; Epay, seven units*

41. Note that this is exactly the least-costly alternative found in Procedure 29, which we already know leads to only five units of waste reaching Kleenville. This means if a pollution-control agency adjusts penalties based on the different impacts, the response by the companies will assure that the least-costly alternative will occur.

CLOSURE

42. Use the following questions to review the key points of the lesson:

A. Give some examples of physical processes that help reduce the impact of waste on the environment. *Dilution and decomposition*

B. What is pollution? *The direct or indirect process resulting from human action by which any part of the environment is made potentially or actually unhealthy, unsafe or hazardous to the welfare of organisms that live in it*

C. What is a flow map? *A map with arrows and lines showing how something moves or diffuses*

D. Generally speaking, how does the distance between the location where waste is put into the environment and the location where it is monitored affect its impact at the monitored location? *The larger the distance between locations, the less the impact*

E. How can waste be reduced? *Install pollution-control equipment, treat the waste, improve the efficiency of production processes, change the nature of the inputs used or outputs produced*

F. Are the costs of reducing waste the same for all companies? *No, some may have processes that are easier and less-expensive to adjust.*

G. Define least-costly alternative. *The alternative that achieves a given objective at the lowest cost, also called the cost-effective choice*

H. What economic and geographic factors should a pollution-control agency consider when determining the least-costly way to meet an environmental goal? *Economic: the cost to each source of reducing waste. Geographic: the location of these sources and the physical*

processes at work in the environment

I. If a pollution-control agency selects the least-costly way to meet an environmental goal, which companies or sources of waste will typically reduce more? *The companies or sources that have lower costs to clean up or control their waste and are located closer to where the goal must be met*

J. What are incentives? *Rewards or penalties that influence people's choices and behaviors*

K. What incentive do companies or other sources of waste have when faced with charges for putting their waste into the environment? *They have the incentive to clean up all the units of waste that are cheaper to control than paying the charge.*

L. Assume a pollution-control agency charges companies for putting waste into the environment. If the agency wants to meet an environmental goal that requires more waste reduction, how should the agency adjust the charge? *It should raise the charge.*

ASSESSMENT

Distribute a copy of Activity 9.3. Review the instructions with the students. When they have completed the activity, go over the answers with them.

1. Why does the location where waste enters a river influence the impact of the waste downstream? *Because of dilution and decomposition — physical forces that act on waste as it moves downstream. The further the waste moves in the river, the more time for dilution and decomposition. The more dilution and decomposition that occurs, the less waste downstream.*

2. The Appleville city council is concerned about waste in the river, much of which comes from companies upstream from Appleville. What economic and geographic factors should the council members think

about as they decide how to clean up the waste in the river? *Economic factors are the cost each company must pay to reduce the amount of waste it puts into the river. Geographic factors are the locations of the companies and how much dilution and decomposition would occur between Appleville and the place where each of the companies puts its waste in the river.*

VISUAL 9.1
FLOW MAP

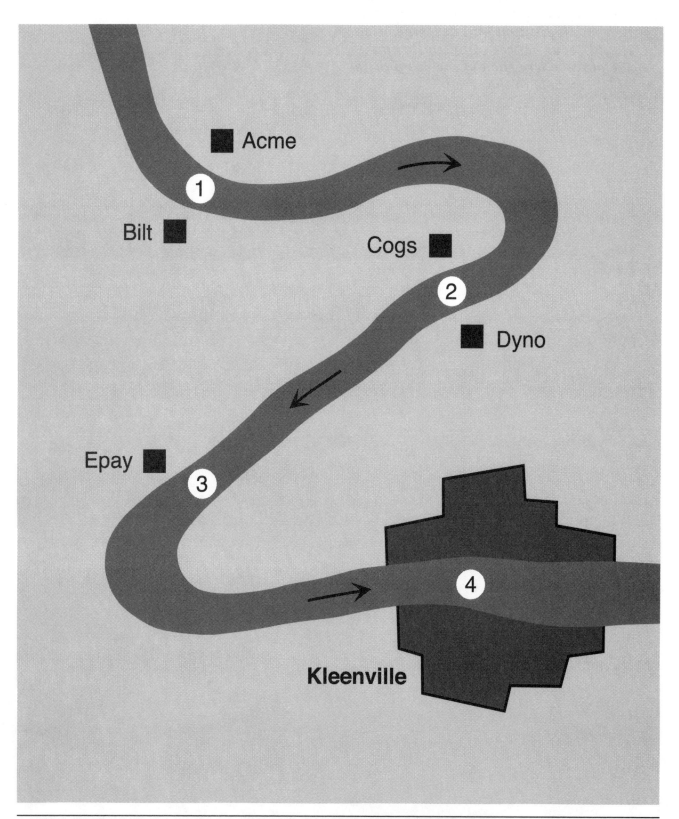

VISUAL 9.2
THE LEAST-COSTLY ALTERNATIVE TO REDUCE WASTE

	Acme	Bilt	Cogs	Dyno	Epay
1st unit	$1	$1	$1	$1	$1
2nd unit	2	1	2	2	1
3rd unit	3	1	3	3	1
4th unit	4	2	4	4	2
5th unit	5	3	5	5	3
6th unit	7	4	7	7	4
7th unit	9	4	9	9	4
8th unit	12	5	12	12	5

The table above shows the costs of reducing waste for each of the five companies upstream from Kleenville. Remember that because of the dilution and
decomposition processes, one-eighth of the waste Acme and Bilt put into the
river reaches Kleenville, one-fourth of the waste from Cogs and Dyno reaches Kleenville and one-half of the waste from Epay reaches Kleenville.

In class you saw that if all five companies reduced their waste by one-half
(from eight units to four), the total waste reaching Kleenville would be cut to
five units. You also saw that this would cost the companies a total of $40.

Here is your task for homework: Instead of requiring each company to
reduce its waste by four units, see if you can find another alternative that
not only cuts the amount of waste reaching Kleenville to five units but also
costs less than a total of $40.

ACTIVITY 9.1
COMPANY COST SHEETS

Your company, **Acme**, creates eight units of waste a day. Here is the cost of reducing each unit of waste:

1st unit:	$1
2nd unit:	$2
3rd unit:	$3
4th unit:	$4
5th unit:	$5
6th unit:	$7
7th unit:	$9
8th unit:	$12

So, for example, to reduce your waste by three units would cost
$1 + $2 + $3 = $6

Your company, **Bilt**, creates eight units of waste a day. Here is the cost of reducing each unit of waste:

1st unit:	$1
2nd unit:	$1
3rd unit:	$1
4th unit:	$2
5th unit:	$3
6th unit:	$4
7th unit:	$4
8th unit:	$5

So, for example, to reduce your waste by three units would cost
$1 + $1 + $1 = $3

ACTIVITY 9.1 (continued)
COMPANY COST SHEETS

Your company, **Cogs**, creates eight units of waste a day. Here is the cost of reducing each unit of waste:
 	
  1st unit: $1
  2nd unit: $2
  3rd unit: $3
  4th unit: $4
  5th unit: $5
  6th unit: $7
  7th unit: $9
  8th unit: $12
 	
So, for example, to reduce your waste by three units would cost
$1 + $2 + $3 = $6
	Your company, **Dyno**, creates eight units of waste a day. Here is the cost of reducing each unit of waste:
	
	  1st unit: $1
	  2nd unit: $2
	  3rd unit: $3
	  4th unit: $4
	  5th unit: $5
	  6th unit: $7
	  7th unit: $9
	  8th unit: $12
	
	So, for example, to reduce your waste by three units would cost
	$1 + $2 + $3 = $6

ACTIVITY 9.1 (continued)
COMPANY COST SHEETS

Your company, **Epay**, creates eight units of waste a day. Here is the cost of reducing each unit of waste:

1st unit:	$1
2nd unit:	$1
3rd unit:	$1
4th unit:	$2
5th unit:	$3
6th unit:	$4
7th unit:	$4
8th unit:	$5

So, for example, to reduce your waste by three units would cost
$1 + $1 + $1 = $3

ACTIVITY 9.2
SEARCHING FOR A LESS-COSTLY ALTERNATIVE

	Acme	Bilt	Cogs	Dyno	Epay
1st unit	$1	$1	$1	$1	$1
2nd unit	2	1	2	2	1
3rd unit	3	1	3	3	1
4th unit	4	2	4	4	2
5th unit	5	3	5	5	3
6th unit	7	4	7	7	4
7th unit	9	4	9	9	4
8th unit	12	5	12	12	5

The costs of reducing waste for each of the five companies upstream from Kleenville are shown in the table above. Remember that because of the dilution and decomposition processes, one-eighth of the waste Acme and Bilt put into the river reaches Kleenville, one-fourth of the waste from Cogs and Dyno reaches Kleenville and one-half of the waste from Epay reaches Kleenville.

In class you saw that if all five companies reduced their waste by one-half (from eight units to four), the total waste reaching Kleenville would be cut to five units. You also saw that this would cost the companies a total of $40.

Here is your task for homework: Instead of having each company reduce its waste by four units, see if you can find another alternative that not only reduces the amount of waste reaching Kleenville to five units but also costs less than a total of $40.

Practice with different alternatives. When you decide on the alternative that you think is best, complete the following information about your alternative:

	Acme	Bilt	Cogs	Dyno	Epay
Number of waste units reduced					
Waste that reaches Kleenville					
Cost to each company					

Total cost of reducing waste: _____

Total amount of waste reaching Kleenville: _____

ACTIVITY 9.3
ASSESSMENT

Read each question and write a brief answer.

1. Why does the location where waste enters a river influence the impact of the waste downstream?

2. The Appleville city council is concerned about waste in the river, much of which comes from by companies upstream from Appleville. What economic and geographic factors should the council members think about as they decide how to clean up the waste in the river?

Glossary of Terms

Absolute advantage: the ability to produce a good or service using the least amount of resources (Lesson 6)

Average years of schooling: average years of schooling received by adults over the age of 15 (Lesson 3)

Benefits: the advantages of a particular course of action as measured by good feelings, dollars or number of items (Lesson 4)

Biome: areas or regions on the Earth with similar climate, plants and animals (Lesson 7)

Capital goods (resources): goods people make and use to produce other goods and services (Lessons 1, 7, 8)

Choropleth maps: maps that display data by political boundary (Lesson 5)

Comparative advantage: the ability to produce a good or service at a lower opportunity cost – that is, by giving up the least amount of other goods and services (Lesson 6)

Continental drift: the movement of continents associated with the movement of tectonic plates (Lesson 6)

Costs: the disadvantages of a particular course of action as measured by bad feelings, dollars or numbers of items (Lesson 4)

Demographers: people who study how population is distributed spatially and by gender, age, occupation and other indicators (Lesson 3)

Development: the process of improvement in the material conditions of people through diffusion of knowledge and technology (Lesson 5)

Earthquake: vibrations and shock waves resulting from the sudden movement of tectonic plates against each other along faults (Lesson 6)

Economic freedom: freedom for consumers to decide how to spend or save their incomes, for workers to change jobs or join unions and for people to establish new businesses or close old ones (Lesson 5)

Flow map: a map with arrows and lines showing how something moves or diffuses (Lesson 9)

Gross domestic product: the market value of all final goods and services produced in a country in one year (Lessons 3, 5)

Gross domestic product per capita: the market value of all final goods and services produced in a country in one year divided by the population of that country (Lessons 3, 5)

Human capital: the quality of labor resources, which can be improved through investments in education, training and health (Lessons 3, 8)

Human resources: the quantity and quality of human effort directed toward producing goods and services (Lessons 1, 7)

Immigrants: people who move into a location, to which they are not native, with the intent of staying for a long period of time (Lesson 4)

Incentive: a reward or penalty that can influence people's choices and behavior (Lesson 9)

Increasing productivity: an increase in the amount of output each worker produces. Increases in productivity occur as a result of specialization, division of labor, investment in human capital and investment in capital goods. (Lesson 8)

Infant mortality: the number of babies who die out of every 1,000 live births (Lessons 3, 5)

Isolines: lines on a map that connect locations with the same amount or level of some physical characteristic (Lesson 2)

Least-costly alternative: the alternative that achieves a given objective at the lowest cost (also called the "cost-effective" choice) (Lesson 9)

Less-developed countries: countries that are changing from uneven growth to more-constant economic conditions and that are generally characterized by low rates of urbanization, relatively high rates of infant mortality and relatively high rates of illiteracy (Lesson 5)

Life expectancy: the number of years an individual is expected to live at birth (Lesson 3)

Literacy rate: the percentage of people over 15 years of age who can read and write (Lessons 3, 5)

Map: diagrams that can be used to show various physical features about a country, state or region (Lessons 1, 2, 9)

Migration: the act of moving from one place to another with the intent of staying permanently or for a relatively long period of time (Lesson 4)

More-developed countries: countries that are technically advanced, highly urbanized and wealthy, and have many manufacturing and service industries (Lesson 5)

Natural resources: "gifts of nature" such as land; these resources are present without human intervention (Lesson 1)

Nonrenewable resources: materials that humans cannot create and therefore cannot replenish. Fossil fuels, nuclear fuels and minerals are examples. Some nonrenewable resources can be reused when recycled, such as aluminum, lead, zinc, diamonds or petroleum by-products. (Lesson 1)

Opportunity cost: the highest-valued alternative people give up when they make a choice (Lessons 2, 6, 7)

Physical environment categories: categories that divide the physical environment into biomes. Categories include deciduous forests, deserts, plains, tundra, savannahs and rainforests. (Lesson 7)

Physical process: a course or method of operation that produces, maintains or alters Earth's physical systems (Lesson 9)

Place: area characterized by physical properties such as climate and soil, vegetation and animal life (Lesson 7)

Pollution: the direct or indirect process resulting from human action by which any part of the environment is made potentially or actually unhealthy, unsafe or hazardous to the welfare of the organisms that live in it (Lesson 9)

Population pyramid: a bar graph showing the distribution, by gender and age, of a region's or country's population (Lesson 3)

Primary, secondary and tertiary economic activity: primary is mainly agriculture, secondary is manufacturing and tertiary is service industries (Lesson 5)

Productivity (labor productivity): the amount of a good or service a worker can produce during a given time period (Lessons 3, 8)

Production possibilities: a table or curve that shows the various combinations of two goods it is possible to produce with a given amount of resources (Lessons 2, 6)

Productive resources: all natural resources, human resources and human-made capital goods (resources) used in the production of goods and services (Lessons 1, 7)

Pull factors: the social, political, economic and environmental attractions that draw people to a new location (Lesson 4)

Push factors: the social, political, economic and environmental factors that force people to move from a location (Lesson 4)

Region: an area that has one or more features in common (Lessons 2, 7)

Relative location: the position of a place in relation to the positions of other places (Lesson 9)

Renewable resources: materials that can be regenerated in nature as fast or faster than society uses them. These materials can be used over and over, and supplies are not depleted. Another kind of renewable resource is perpetual resources. These come from sources that are virtually inexhaustible, such as the sun, wind, waves, tides and geothermal energy. (Lesson 1)

Rift: a large crack or fault in the earth's surface (Lesson 6)

Scale: the relationship between a linear measurement on a map and the corresponding distance on the Earth's surface (Lesson 2)

Scarcity: the condition that exists when people's wants exceed the resources available to satisfy their wants (Lesson 1)

Specialization: concentrating on the production of one or a few goods as opposed to producing all the goods that people desire (Lesson 6)

Spider graphs: data points plotted on a grid with a number of axes, each with its own scale. Drawing a line that connects the points creates a shape that shows a relationship among the data. (Lesson 3)

Standard of living: goods and services per person in a country; measured by gross domestic product per capita (Lessons 3, 5, 8)

Technological change: an advance in knowledge that leads to new and improved goods and services and better ways of producing them (Lesson 8)

Tectonic plates: sections of the Earth's crust that move as distinct units over the Earth's mantle (Lesson 6)

Wants: desires that can be satisfied by consuming goods and services (Lesson 1)